RED ROSES FOR ME

BOOKS BY SEAN O'CASEY

Plays

Two Plays
Juno and the Paycock
The Plough and the Stars
Within the Gates
The Star Turns Red
Purple Dust
Five Irish Plays

Biography

I Knock at the Door
Pictures in the Hallway

General

The Flying Wasp:
Comments on the Present-
day Theatre
Windfalls: Verses, Stories, and
One-Act Plays

RED ROSES
FOR ME

A Play in Four Acts

BY

SEAN O'CASEY

" You may break, you may shatter the vase, if you will,
But the scent of the roses will hang round it still."

NEW YORK
THE MACMILLAN COMPANY
1944

Copyright, 1943, by

SEAN O'CASEY.

FIRST PRINTING.

SECOND PRINTING.

PRINTED IN THE UNITED STATES OF AMERICA

*My thanks to Brigid Edwards
for setting down the airs to
the songs*

CHARACTERS IN THE PLAY

MRS. BREYDON

AYAMONN BREYDON, *her son*

EEADA
DYMPNA } *Mrs. Breydon's neighbours in the house*
FINNOOLA

SHEILA MOORNEEN, *Ayamonn's sweetheart*

BRENNAN O' THE MOOR, *Owner of a few oul' houses*

A SINGER, *A young man with a good voice*

ROORY O'BALACAUN, *A zealous Irish Irelander*

MULLCANNY, *A mocker of sacred things*

REV. E. CLINTON, *Rector of St. Burnupus*

SAMUEL, *Sexton to the church*

INSPECTOR FINGLAS, *Of the Mounted Police, and the Rector's churchwarden*

1ST MAN
2ND MAN } *Neighbours in the next house to Breydons'*
3RD MAN

DOWZARD
FOSTER } *Members of St. Burnupus' Select Vestry*

A LAMPLIGHTER

1ST RAILWAYMAN.

2ND RAILWAYMAN.

SCENES

I.—Two-roomed home of the Breydons.

II.—The same.

III.—A Dublin street, beside a bridge over the river Liffey.

IV.—Part of the grounds round the Protestant Church of St. Burnupus. In this Act the curtain is lowered for a few minutes to denote the passing of a few hours.

TIME.—A little while ago.

ACT I

Scene : *The front one of two rather dilapidated
rooms in a poor working-class locality. The
walls, whitewashed, are dwindling into a
rusty yellowish tinge. The main door, leading
to the hall, is at the back, a little towards the
right. The fireplace is in the right-hand wall,
and a brilliant fire is burning in the large,
old-fashioned grate. In the centre of the room
is an old ebony-hued table on which stands a
one-wick oil-lamp, its chimney a little smoky
from the bad oil in the reservoir. Some books
lie on the table, some paper, coloured chalks,
a pen, and a small bottle of ink. In the left
wall, up towards the back, is the door leading
to the second room. Below this door is a
horsehair sofa showing signs of old age. On
it, to the head, is a neatly folded bundle of
sheets and blankets, showing that it is used
as a bed during the night. To the left of the
main door at back is a large basket used by
actors when on tour. On the other side of
this door is an ordinary kitchen dresser on
which some of the crockery is on the ledge,
for the upper shelf is filled with a row of
books, by the look of them second-hand. Over
the basket, on the wall, is tacked a childlike,
brightly-coloured pastel of what is meant to be a
copy of one of Fra Angelico's angels blowing a*

1

curved and golden trumpet ; and beside it is a small coloured reproduction of Constable's " Cornfield ". In the same wall, towards the back, is a large, tall window, nearly reaching the ceiling, and, when one is in front of it, the top of a railway signal, with transverse arms, showing green and red lights, can be seen. Under this window, on a roughly made bench, stand three biscuit tins. In the first grows a geranium, in the second, musk, and in the third, a fuchsia. The disks of the geranium are extremely large and glowing ; the tubular blooms of the golden musk, broad, gay, and rich ; and the purple bells of the fuchsia, surrounded by their long white waxy sepals, seem to be as big as arum lilies. These crimson, gold, and purple flowers give a regal tint to the poor room. Occasionally in the distance can be heard the whistle of an engine, followed by its strenuous puffing as it pulls at a heavy rake of goods wagons. A chair or two stand about the room.

It is towards the evening of a mid-spring day, and the hour would make it dusk, but it is darker than that, for the sky is cloudy and rain is falling heavily over the city.

AYAMONN and his mother are in the room when the scene shows itself. He is tall, well built, twenty-two or so, with deep brown eyes, fair hair, rather bushy, but tidily kept, and his face would remind an interested observer of a rather handsome, firm-minded, thoughtful,

2

and good-humoured bulldog. His mother is coming up to fifty, her face brownish, dark eyes with a fine glint in them, and she bears on her cheeks and brow the marks of struggle and hard work. She is dressed in a black jacket, fitting close, marred by several patches, done very neatly, dark-blue skirt, a little faded, and rather heavily-soled boots. At the moment this is all covered with a rich blue velvet cloak, broidered with silver lace, and she is sitting on a kitchen chair covered with a dark-red, rather ragged cloth.

AYAMONN *wears a bright green silk doublet over which is a crimson velvet armless cloak bordered with white fur. The back part of the cloak is padded so as to form a big hump between his shoulders. Across his chest is a dark-green baldric from which hangs a scabbard. A cross-hilted sword is in his hand. On his head he has a black felt hat with narrow turned-up rims. A black band goes round the hat, and a crimson feather sticks up from it. His legs are in heavy, black, working corduroy trousers, and he wears heavy hobnailed boots. She and he are in an intently listening attitude.*

MRS. BREYDON
(*whispering over to* AYAMONN)

She's gone; wanted to borra something else, I suppose. They're feverish with borrowing in this blessed house !

3

Damn her for a troublesome fool ! Where's this
I was when the knock came ?

I was just goin' to say
  Ay, an' for much more slaughter after this,
  O God ! forgive my sins, and pardon thee !

(looking at the floor)

Oh yes ! *(He recites)*—
  What, will th' aspiring blood of Lancaster
  Sink to the ground ? I thought it would have
    mounted.
  (He holds the sword aloft, and stares at it) See
    how my sword weeps for the poor king's
    death !
  O, may such purple tears be always shed
  For those that wish the downfall of our house !
  If any spark of life be yet remaining,
  (He stabs at the floor) Down, down to hell ; and
    say I sent thee thither !
    [*A knuckle-knock is heard at the door.*
    AYAMONN *and* MRS. BREYDON *stiffen into a
    silent listening attitude. A fine baritone
    voice, husky with age, is heard speaking
    outside.*

Is anyone in or out or what ? *(Louder raps are
given as* AYAMONN *steals over, and places his back*

4

to the door.) Eh, in there — is there anyone movin', or is the oul' shack empty ?

MRS. BREYDON
(*in a whisper*)

Oul' Brennan on the Moor. He was here before, today. He's got his rent for his oul' houses, an' he wants to be told again that the Bank of Ireland's a safe place to put it.

AYAMONN
(*warningly*)

Ssshush !

VOICE

No answer, eh ? An' me afther seein' a light in th' window. Maybe they are out. For their own sakes, I hope they are ; for it's hardly an honourable thing to gainsay a neighbour's knock.

[*The sound of feet shuffling away is heard outside, and then there is silence for a few moments.*

MRS. BREYDON

He's gone. He's always a bit lively the day he gets his rents. How a man, with his money, can go on livin' in two rooms in a house an' sthreet only a narrow way betther than this, I don't know. What was he but an oul' painter an' paperhanger, starvin' to save, an' usin' his cunnin' to buy up a few oul' houses, give them a lick o' paint, and charge the highest rent for th' inconvenience of living' in them !

AYAMONN

I wish he'd keep himself and his throubles far

5

away from me now. I've higher things to think of and greater things to do than to be attached to the agony of an old fool for ever afraid a fistful of money'll be snatched away from him. Still, he isn't a miser, for he gives kids toys at Christmas, and never puts less than half a crown on the plate in church on Sundays.

MRS. BREYDON

So well he may !

AYAMONN

What was he sayin' when he was here before ?

MRS. BREYDON

Oh, th' usual question of askin' me what I thought about the Bank of Ireland ; mutterin' about somebody not payin' the rent ; and that his birthday's due tomorrow.

AYAMONN

(*looking at the chair*)

I'll have to get a loan of a chair with arms on, and someway make them golden to do the thing proper in the Temperance Hall ; and I'll paint for the back of it, on thin cardboard, a cunning design of the House of Lancaster, the red rose, so that it'll look like a kingly seat.

MRS. BREYDON

Th' killin' o' th' king be th' Duke o' Gloster should go down well, an' th' whole thing should look sumptuous.

AYAMONN

So it will. It's only that they're afraid of Shakespeare out of all that's been said of him. They
think he's beyond them, while all the time he's
part of the kingdom of heaven in the nature of
everyman. Before I'm done, I'll have him
drinking in th' pubs with them !

MRS. BREYDON

I don't know that he'll go well with a Minstrel
Show.

AYAMONN

He'll have to go well. If only King Henry
doesn't rant too much, saw the air with his hands,
and tear his passion to tatthers. The old fool
saw someone do it that way, and thinks it must
be right. (*With a sigh.*) I daren't attempt to
recite my part now, for Oul' Brennan on the
Moor's waitin' and listenin' somewhere down
below ; so I'll just get it off by heart. How old
does he say he'll be tomorrow ?

MRS. BREYDON

Only seventy-six, he says, an' feelin' as if he was
lookin' forward to his twenty-first birthday.

AYAMONN

Well, he won't have long to wait.

MRS. BREYDON
(*slyly*)

He was muttherin', too, about some air or other
on the oul' piano he has at home.

7

AYAMONN

(*springing up from where he has been sitting*)
It's one o' mine he's put an air to ! (*He rushes
from the room and returns in a few moments.*)
He's not there ; gone home, I suppose. ﹍ ﹍ ﹍
I wish you's told me that at first.

MRS. BREYDON

I'd thry to rest a little, Ayamonn, before you go
to work. You're overdoing it. Less than two
hours' sleep today, and a long night's work
before you. Sketchin', readin', makin' songs, an'
learnin' Shakespeare : if you had a piano, you'd
be thryin' to learn music. Why don't you stick
at one thing, an' leave the others alone ?

AYAMONN

They are all lovely, and my life needs them all.

MRS. BREYDON

I managed to get on well enough without them.
(*A pause. She goes over to the window, and
tenderly touches the fuchsia.*) There's this sorry-
ful sthrike, too, about to come down on top of us.

AYAMONN

(*sitting in the red-covered chair and reading
Shakespeare — quietly and confidently*)
There'll be no strike. The bosses won't fight.
They'll grant the extra shilling a week demanded.

MRS. BREYDON

(*now fingering the musk*)
I thought this Minstrel Show was being run to
gather funds together ?

8

AYAMONN

(*impatiently*)

So it is, so it is ; but only in case the strike may
have to take place. I haven't much to do with
it, anyway. I'm with the men, spoke at a meeting
in favour of the demand, and that's all.

MRS. BREYDON

You'll undhermine your health with all you're
doin', tearin' away what's left of your time be
runnin' afther—— (*She checks herself, and
becomes silent.*)

AYAMONN

(*lowering his book to his lap — angrily*)

Go on — finish what you started to say : runnin'
afther who ?

MRS. BREYDON

Nobody, nobody.

AYAMONN

Runnin' afther Sheila Moorneen — that's what
was in your mind to say, wasn't it ?

MRS. BREYDON

If it was aself ; is there a new law out that a
body's not to think her own thoughts ?

AYAMONN

(*sharply*)

What have you got against the girl ?

MRS. BREYDON

Nothing. As a girl, I'd say she's a fine coloured

9

silken shawl among a crowd of cotton ones. A
girl I'd say could step away from the shadowy
hedges where others slink along, tiltin' her head
as she takes the centre of the road for the enther-
prisin' light o' day to show her off to everyone.
Still—— (*She stops speaking again.*)

AYAMONN

Ay, but still what? You've a maddenin' way of
never finishing some of your sentences.

MRS. BREYDON
(*braving it out*)

She's a Roman Catholic; steeped in it, too, the
way she'd never forgive a one for venturin' to
test the Pope's pronouncement.

AYAMONN

And who wants to test the Pope's pronouncement?
Life and all her vital changes'll go on testing
everything, even to the Pope's pronouncement.
D'ye think I've laboured as I have, and am
labourin' now, to furnish myself with some of the
greatness of the mighty minds of the past, just to
sink down into passive acceptance of the Pope's
pronouncement? Let the girl believe what she
may, reverence what she can : it's her own use
of her own mind. That she is fair to look upon,
charming to talk with, and a dear companion, is
well and away enough for me, were she even a
believer in Mumbo Jumbo, and had a totem pole
in her front garden.

MRS. BREYDON

There's worse still than that in it.

AYAMONN

Worse, is there ?   An' what may that be ?

MRS. BREYDON

She's th' child of a sergeant in the Royal Irish
Constabulary, isn't she ?

AYAMONN

Well, she can't help it, can she ?

MRS. BREYDON

I know that ; but many have murmured again' a
son of mine goin' with the child of a man crouchin'
close to their enemy.

AYAMONN

Everything, it seems, is against her, save herself.
I like herself, and not her faith ; I want herself,
and not her father.

MRS. BREYDON

The bigger half of Ireland would say that a man's
way with a maid must be regulated by his faith
an' hers, an' the other half by the way her father
makes his livin'.

AYAMONN

And let the whole world join them !   Fair she is,
and her little ear's open to hear all that I thry
to say, so, were she the child of darkness aself,
I'd catch her hand and lead her out and show her
off to all men.

MRS. BREYDON

She wouldn't be a lot to look at afther she'd wended her way through poverty with you for a year an' a day.

AYAMONN

She gives no honour to gold ; neither does her warm heart pine for silks and satins from China and Japan, or the spicy isles of Easthern Asia. A sober black shawl on her shoulders, a simple petticoat, and naked feet would fail to find her craving finer things that envious women love.

MRS. BREYDON

Ah, go on with you, Ayamonn, for a kingly fool. I'm tellin' you th' hearts of all proper girls glow with the dhream of fine things ; an' I'm tellin' you, too, that the sword jinglin' on th' hip of Inspector Finglas, the red plume hangin' from his menacin' helmet, an' th' frosty silver sparklin' on his uniform, are a dazzle o' light between her tantalised eyes an' whatever she may happen to see in you.

AYAMONN

Tell me something else to add to my hope.

MRS. BREYDON

Go on readin', an' don't bother to listen to your mother.

AYAMONN

(*going over and gently putting his hands on her shoulders*)

I do listen, but I am drifting away from you,

Mother, a dim shape now, in a gold canoe, dipping over a far horizon.

MRS. BREYDON
(*with a catch in her voice*)
I did an' dared a lot for you, Ayamonn, my son, in my time, when jeerin' death hurried your father off to Heaven.

AYAMONN
It's I who know that well : when it was dark, you always carried the sun in your hand for me ; when you suffered me to starve rather than thrive towards death in an Institution, you gave me life to play with as a richer child is given a coloured ball. (*He gently lifts up her face by putting a hand under her chin.*) The face, the dear face that once was smooth is wrinkled now ; the eyes, brown still, that once were bright, have now been dimmed by a sthrained stare into the future ; the sturdy back that stood so straight, is bending. A well-tried leaf, bronzed with beauty, waiting for a far-off winter wind to shake it from the tree.

MRS. BREYDON
(*gently removing his hand from her chin*)
I have a tight hold still. My back can still bear many a heavy burden ; and my eyes, dimmer now than once they were, can still see far enough. Well, I betther take this fancy robe from off me, lest it give me gorgeous notions.
[*She takes off her robe, and leaves it carefully folded on the basket, then goes over and*

13

arranges the fire. AYAMONN *looks thought-fully out of the window, then takes off cloak, sword, and hat, leaving them carefully on the basket.*

AYAMONN
(*musingly*)

He'll hardly come tonight in this rain. If he does, I'll get him to read the King's part, and do mine over again.

MRS. BREYDON

Who's to come tonight ?

AYAMONN

Mullcanny : he's searching Dublin for a book he wants to give me ; and, if he got it, he was to bring it tonight — *The Riddle of the Universe*.

MRS. BREYDON

That's another one I wouldn't see too much of, for he has the whole neighbourhood up in arms against his reckless disregard of God, an' his mockery of everything solemn, set down as sacred.

AYAMONN

Oh, Tim is all right. The people are sensible enough to take all he says in good part ; and a black flame stands out in a brightly-coloured world.

MRS. BREYDON

You don't know them, if you say that ; he'll meet with a mishap, some day, if he doesn't keep his mouth shut.

14

Nonsense.

[*She has quietly slipped a shawl around her,
and is moving to the door so silently as to
seem to want to prevent* AYAMONN *from
noticing her movements, when the door
opens and* EEADA, DYMPNA, FINNOOLA, *and
several men, appear there. The three
women come a little way into the room;
the men stay around the door. All their
faces are stiff and mask-like, holding tight
an expression of dumb resignation; and
are traversed with seams of poverty and a
hard life. The face of* EEADA *is that of an
old woman; that of* DYMPNA, *one coming
up to middle age; and that of* FINNOOLA,
*one of a young girl. Each shows the
difference of age by more or less furrows,
but each has the same expressionless stare
out on life.*

DYMPNA *is carrying a statue of the Blessed
Virgin, more than two feet high, in her
arms. The figure was once a glory of
purest white, sparkling blue, and luscious
gilding; but the colours have faded, the
gilt is gone, save for a spot or two of dull
gold still lingering on the crown. She is
wearing a crown that, instead of being
domed, is castellated like a city's tower,
resembling those of Dublin; and the pale
face of the Virgin is sadly soiled by the
grime of the house. The men are dressed in*

15

drab brown, the women in a chill grey, each
suit or dress having a patch of faded blue,
red, green, or purple somewhere about them.

EEADA
(*to* MRS. BREYDON)

Could you spare a pinch or two of your Hudson's
soap, Mrs. Breydon, dear, to give the Blessed
Virgin a bit of a wash? (*To all in general*)
Though I've often said it's th' washin' that's
done away with the bonnie blue of th' robe an'
th' braver gold of its bordhers an' th' most o' th'
royalty outa th' crown. Little Ursula below's
savin' up her odd pennies to bring Her where
She'll find a new blue robe, an' where they'll
make the royalty of th' gilt glow again ; though
whenever she's a shillin' up, it's needed for food
an' firin' ; but we never yet found Our Lady of
Eblana averse to sellin' Her crown an' Her blue
robe to provide for Her people's need. (MRS.
BREYDON *gives her half a packet of soap powder.*
Gratefully) Thank you, ma'am, an' though y'are
of a different persuasion, Our Blessed Lady of
Eblana's poor'll bless you an' your fine son for
this little tribute to Her honour and circumspect
appearance before the world.

THE REST
(*murmuring*)

Ay will She, an' that's a sure thing.
  [*They open a way for* EEADA *to pass out, with*
     DYMPNA *carrying the statue, following in a*

16

kind of a simple procession. MRS. BREYDON
is moving slowly after them.

AYAMONN
(*who has noticed her under his eyes*)
You're not going out again, surely — on a night
like this, too ?

MRS. BREYDON
Not really ; only down the road to Mrs. Cash-
more's. She's not too well ; I promised I'd dhrop
in, and see to a hot dhrink or something for her
before she wandhered off to sleep.

AYAMONN
(*irritably*)
You think more of other homes than you do of
your own ! Every night for the past week you've
been going out on one silly mission or another
like an imitation sisther of charity.

MRS. BREYDON
I couldn't sit quiet knowin' the poor woman
needed me. I'd hear her voice all through the
night complainin' I never came to give her a hot
dhrink, settle her bed soft, an' make her safe for
th' lonely hours of th' slow-movin' night.

AYAMONN
A lot they'd do for you if you happened to need
help from them.

MRS. BREYDON
Ah, we don't know. A body shouldn't think of
that, for such a belief would dismay an' dismantle

17

everything done outside of our own advantage.
No harm to use an idle hour to help another in
need.

AYAMONN

An' wear yourself out in the process ?

MRS. BREYDON
(with a sigh)

I 'll wear out, anyway, sometime, an' a tired ould
body can, at least, go to its long rest without any
excuse.

> [*As she opens the door to go out,* SHEILA
> *appears on the threshold. She is a girl of
> about twenty-three, fairly tall, a fine figure,
> carrying herself with a sturdiness never
> ceasing to be graceful. She has large,
> sympathetic brown eyes, that dim, now and
> again, with a cloud of timidity. Her mouth
> is rather large, but sweetly made ; her hair
> is brown and long, though now it is gathered
> up into a thick coil that rests on the nape
> of her neck. She is dressed in a tailor-made
> suit of rich brown tweed, golden-brown
> blouse, and a bright-blue hat. These are
> now covered with a fawn-coloured mackin-
> tosh, darkened with heavy rain, and a hastily
> folded umbrella is dripping on to the floor.
> She comes in shyly, evidently conscious of*
> MRS. BREYDON's *presence ; but fighting her
> timidity with a breezy and jovial demeanour.*
> MRS. BREYDON *tries, but can't keep a little
> stiffness out of her greeting.*

SHEILA

Oh! good evening, Mrs. Breydon. What a
night! I'm nearly blown to bits; and the rain
— oh, the wind and the weather!

MRS. BREYDON

You must be perished. Take off your mac, and
come over to the fire. Get Ayamonn to make
you a cup o' tea, and bring you back to life again.

SHEILA

No, really; I'm burning — the battle with the
wind and the rain has made me warm and lively.

AYAMONN

Hey ho, the wind and the rain, for the rain it
raineth every day. Sit down and take the weight
off your legs.

SHEILA

Not worth while, for I can't stop long. (*To* MRS.
BREYDON) Going out on a night like this, Mrs.
Breydon?

AYAMONN
(hastily)

She has to go: got an urgent call from a poor
sick neighbour.

SHEILA
(hesitatingly)

What is it? Could . . . could I do it for you?

AYAMONN
(decidedly)

No, no, you couldn't. The woman knows my

mother. It's only to see her safe and warm in
bed for the night ; Mother won't be long.

MRS. BREYDON

Good night, Miss Sheila ; perhaps you'll be here
when I come back.

SHEILA

I don't think so.   I must go almost at once.

MRS. BREYDON

Well, good night, then.
[*She goes out, and* AYAMONN *goes over to*
SHEILA, *kisses her, and helps her off with
the mac.*

SHEILA

You shouldn't let your mother go out on a night
like this — she's no longer a young woman.

AYAMONN

I don't like to interfere with her need to give help
to a neighbour.   She likes it, and it does her good.

SHEILA

But the rain's coming down in sheets, and she's
got but a thin shawl round her shoulders.

AYAMONN

(*impatiently*)

Oh, she hasn't very far to go.   Let's think of
greater things than the pouring rain and an old
woman on her way to smooth pillows on a sick
bed.   Look ! — (*he feels her skirt*) — the hem's
wringing.   Better dry it at the fire.   Turn round
and I'll unfasten it for you.

20

SHEILA

(*forcing his hand away*)

It's nothing — you are thinking now of your own
pleasure.

AYAMONN

(*brightly*)

And so in that way thinking of yours too, I hope.
I never expected you today, and so the pleasure's
doubled.

SHEILA

You weren't so eager to see me when I was
knocking at the door a while ago.

AYAMONN

You!   But it was Old Brennan on the Moor that
was there.

SHEILA

Before him, I was there.   He hammered at the
door too.

AYAMONN

(*angry with himself*)

And I thinking the rapping was that of a pestering
neighbour!   I might have guessed it wasn't, it
was so gentle.

SHEILA

After trying to slip in unnoticed, there I was left
with the whole house knowing I was at the door,
and when I ran down, I heard them yelling that
the stylish-dressed pusher was trying to get into
Breydon's again!   A nice time I'll have with my
people when they hear it.

21

AYAMONN

I was doing my Shakespeare part, and didn't want disturbance, so there I was, standing stiff and breathless like a heron in a pond, keeping my dear one away from me ! (*Going over and taking her in his arms*) Well, it's all over now, and here you are in my arms, safe and sure and lovely.

SHEILA
(*struggling away from him*)
No, it's not all over ; and don't press me so hard ; don't ruffle me tonight, for I feel a little tired.

AYAMONN
(*peevishly*)
Tired again ? Well, so am I, more than a little tired ; but never too tired to put a sparkle into a welcome for a loved one.

SHEILA
Oh, Ayamonn, I do want you to be serious for one night.

AYAMONN
Very well, very well, Sheila. (*He moves away from her, and stands at the other side of the fire.*) Let us plan, then, of how we can spin joy into every moment of tomorrow's day.

SHEILA
That's why I hurried here to see you — I can't be with you tomorrow. (*There is a long pause.*)

AYAMONN
Why can't you be with me tomorrow ?

22

SHEILA

The Daughters of St. Frigid begin a retreat tomorrow, to give the Saint a warm devotion and Mother insists I go.

AYAMONN

And I insist that you go with me. Is the Saint Frigid more to you than the sinner Ayamonn? Would you rather go to the meeting than come to see me? (*A pause.*) Would you, would you, Sheila?

SHEILA

(*in a hesitant whisper*)

God forgive me, I'd rather come to see you.

AYAMONN

Come then; God will be sure to forgive you.

SHEILA

I daren't. My mother would be at me for ever if I failed to go. I've told you how she hates me to be near you. She chatters red-lined warnings and black-bordered appeals into my ears night and day, and when they dwindle for lack of breath, my father shakes them out of their drowsiness and sends them dancing round more lively still, dressed richly up in deadly black and gleaming scarlet.

AYAMONN

Sheila, Sheila, on the one day of the month when I'm free, you must be with me. I wouldn't go to a workers' meeting so that I might be with you.

23

SHEILA

There's another thing, Ayamonn — the threatened strike. Oh, why do you meddle with those sort of things !

AYAMONN

Oh, never mind that, now. Refuse to let yourself be like a timid little girl safely ensconced in a clear space in a thicket of thorns — safe from a scratch if she doesn't stir, but unable to get to the green grass or the open road unless she risks the tears the thorns can give.

SHEILA

Oh, Ayamonn, for my sake, if you love me, do try to be serious.

AYAMONN
(*a little wildly*)

Oh, Sheila, our time is not yet come to be serious in the way of our elders. Soon enough to browse with wisdom when Time's grey finger puts a warning speck on the crimson rose of youth. Let no damned frosty prayer chill the sunny sighs that dread the joy of love.

SHEILA
(*wildly*)

I won't listen, Ayamonn, I won't listen ! We must look well ahead on the road to the future. You lead your life through too many paths instead of treading the one way of making it possible for us to live together.

AYAMONN

We live together now ; live in the light of the burning bush. I tell you life is not one thing, but many things, a wide branching flame, grand and good to see and feel, dazzling to the eye of no-one loving it. I am not one to carry fear about with me as a priest carries the Host. Let the timid tiptoe through the way where the paler blossoms grow ; my feet shall be where the redder roses grow, though they bear long thorns, sharp and piercing, thick among them !

SHEILA

(rising from the chair — vehemently)
I'll listen no more ; I'll go. You want to make me a spark in a mere illusion. I'll go !

AYAMONN

Rather a spark from the althar of God, me girl ; a spark that flames on a new path for a bubbling moment of life, or burns a song into the heart of a poet.

SHEILA

I came here as a last chance to talk things quiet with you, but you won't let me ; so I'll go. (*As he seizes her in his arms*) Let me go ! (*Pleadingly*) Please, Ayamonn, let me go !

AYAMONN

I tell you it is a gay sight for God to see joy shine for a moment on the faces of His much-troubled children. Oh, Sheila, Sheila, to be afraid of love is to be afraid for ever, for it is but the careless murmur of the rushy brook transfigured to a torrent.

SHEILA
(*fearfully*)
Oh, don't bring God's name into this, for it will mean trouble to the pair of us. And your love for me lasts only while I'm here. When I'm gone, you think more of your poor painting, your poor oul' Ireland, your songs, and your workers' union than you think of Sheila.

AYAMONN
You're part of them all, in them all, and through them all ; joyous, graceful, and a dearer vision ; a bonnie rose, delectable and red. (*He draws her to him, presses her hard, lifts her on to his lap, and kisses her.*) Sheila, darling, you couldn't set aside the joy that makes the moon a golden berry in a hidden tree. You cannot close your ear to the sweet sound of the silver bell that strikes but once and never strikes again !

[*The door opens, and the head of* BRENNAN ON THE MOOR *looks into the room. It is a bald one, the dome highly polished ; the face is wrinkled a lot, but the eyes are bright and peering. A long white beard gives him a far-away likeness to St. Jerome. He is dressed in a shabby-genteel way, and wears a long rain-soaked mackintosh. A faded bowler hat is on his head.*

Oh, dear, dear, dear me !

[*He comes into the room showing that his*
back is well bent, though he still has a
sturdy look about him. A strap around his
body holds a melodeon on his back. SHEILA
and AYAMONN *separate ; he rises to meet*
the old man, while she stares, embarrassed,
into the fire.

AYAMONN

Now what th' hell do you want ?

BRENNAN

(*taking no notice of* AYAMONN's *remark—taking*
off his hat in a sweeping bow)

Ah, me two sweet, snowy-breasted Dublin doves !
Me woe it is to come ramblin' in through mar-
joram moments scentin' the serious hilarity of a
genuine courtin' couple. I'm askin' now what's
the dear one's name, if that isn't thresspassin' on
others who are in a firmer condition of friendship ?
Though, be rights, it's a fair an' showy nosegay
I should be throwin' through a shyly opened
window into the adorable lady's lap.

SHEILA
(*shyly*)

Me name is Sheila.

BRENNAN

Sheila is it ? Ay, an' a Sheila are you ? Ay, an'
a suitable one too, for there's a gentle nature in

27

the two soft sounds, an' a silver note in the echo, describin' grandly the pretty slendher lass me two ould eyes are now beholdin'.

AYAMONN

(*going over and catching him by an arm to guide him out*)

I can't see you now, old friend, for the pair of us are heavily harnessed to a question that must be answered before either of us is a day older.

BRENNAN

Sure I know. An' isn't it only natural, too, that young people should have questions to ask and answers to give to the dewy problems that get in th' way of their dancin' feet?

AYAMONN

(*impatiently*)

Come again, old friend, when time has halted us for an hour of rest.

BRENNAN

It isn't me, I'm sayin', that would be dense enough to circumvent your longin' to be deep down in the silent consequence of regardin' each other without let or hindrance. (*He goes towards* SHEILA, *eagerly*, *pulling* AYAMONN *after him.*) It's easy seen, sweet lady, that you're well within the compass of your young man's knowledge, an' unaware of nothin', so I may speak as man to lady, so with cunnin' confidence, tell me what you think of the Bank of Ireland?

28

Oh, for goodness' sake, old man, Sheila's no intherest in the Bank of Ireland. She cares nothing for money, or for anything money can buy.

BRENNAN

(*staring at* AYAMONN *for a moment as if he had received a shock*)

Eh ? Ara, don't be talkin' nonsense, man ! Who is it daren't think of what money can buy ? (*He crosses to the door in a trot on his toes, opens it, looks out, and closes it softly again. Then he tiptoes back to* SHEILA, *bends down towards her, hands on knees, and whispers hoarsely*) I've just a little consideration of stocks and bonds nestin' in the Bank of Ireland, at four per cent — just enough to guard a poor man from ill, eh ? Safe an' sound there, isn't it, eh ? (*To* AYAMONN) Now, let the fair one speak out on her own. (*Twisting his head back to* SHEILA.) Safe there as if St. Pether himself had the key of where the bonds are stationed, eh ?

SHEILA

I'm sure they must be, sir.

BRENNAN

(*with chuckling emphasis*)

Yehess ! Aren't you the sensible young lady ; sure I knew you'd say that, without fear or favour. (*Turning towards* AYAMONN.) What do you say ? You're a man, now, of tellin' judgement.

29

AYAMONN

Oh, the State would have to totther before you'd lose a coin.

BRENNAN
(*gleefully*)

Go bang, absolutely bang ! Eh ?

AYAMONN

Go bang !

BRENNAN

Bang ! (*To* SHEILA) Hear that, now, from a man climbin' up to scholarship ? Yehess ! Stony walls, steely doors, locks an' keys, bolts an' bars, an' all th' bonds warm an' dhry, an' shinin' safe behind them.

SHEILA

Safe behind them.

BRENNAN
(*gleefully*)

Ay, so. An' none of it sthrollin into Peter's Pence. (*Chuckling.*) Wouldn't the Pope be mad if he knew what he was missin' ! Safe an' sound. (*To* AYAMONN) You think so, too, eh ?

AYAMONN

Yes, yes.

BRENNAN
(*soberly*)

Ay, of course you do. (*To* SHEILA — *indicating* AYAMONN) A good breed, me sweet an' fair one, brought up proper to see things in their right light.

30

AYAMONN
(*catching him impatiently by the arm*)
And now, old friend, we have to get you to go.

BRENNAN

Eh ?

AYAMONN
To go ; Sheila and I have things to talk about.

BRENNAN
(*suddenly*)
An' what about the song, then ?

AYAMONN

Song ?

BRENNAN
Th' one for the Show.   Isn't that what brought
me up ?   At long last, afther hard sthrainin', me
an' Sammy have got the tune down in tested
clefs, crotchets, an' quavers, fair set down to be
sung be anyone in thrue time.   An' Sammy's
below, in his gay suit for the Show, waitin' to be
called up to let yous hear th' song sung as only
Sammy can sing it.

AYAMONN
Bring him up, bring him up — why in hell didn't
you tell me all this before ?

BRENNAN
(*stormily*)
Wasn't I thryin' all the time an' you wouldn't let
a man get a word in edgeways.   (*Gesturing*

towards SHEILA.) He'll jib at singin' in front of
her. (*He whispers hoarsely towards* SHEILA.)
He's as shy as a kid in his first pair o' pants,
dear lady.

AYAMONN
(*impatiently pushing him out of the room*)
Oh, go on, go on, man, and bring him up.

[BRENNAN *goes out.*

SHEILA
(*earnestly*)
Wait till I'm gone, Ayamonn ; I can't stop long,
and I want to talk to you so much.

AYAMONN
(*a little excited*)
Oh, you must hear the song, Sheila ; they've
been working to get the air down for a week, and
it won't take a minute.

SHEILA
(*angrily*)
I've waited too long already ! Aren't you more
interested in what I want to say than to be
listening to some vain fool singing a song ?

AYAMONN
(*a little taken aback*)
Oh, Sheila, what's wrong with you tonight ?
The young carpenter who'll sing it, so far from
being vain, is as shy as a field-mouse, and you'll
see, when he starts to sing, he'll edge his face

32

away from us.   You do want to hear it, Sheila, don't you ?

SHEILA
(*appealingly*)

Let it wait over, Ayamonn ;   I can come to hear it some other time.   I do want to say something, very serious, to you about our future meetings.

AYAMONN
(*hastily*)

All right then ;   I'll hurry them off the minute the song's sung.   Here they are, so sit down, do, just for one minute more.

[*But she goes towards the door, and reaches it just as* OLD BRENNAN *returns shoving in before him a young man of twenty-three, shy, and loth to come in.   He is tall, but his face is pale and mask-like in its expression of resignation to the world and all around him.   Even when he shows he's shy, the mask-like features do not alter.   He is dressed in a white cut-away coat, shaped like a tailed evening dress, black waistcoat over a rather soiled shirt-front, frilled, and green trousers.   He carries a sheet of manuscript music in his hand.* BRENNAN *unslings his melodeon from his back, fusses the young* SINGER *forward ; bumping against* SHEILA, *who has moved towards the door, he pushes her back with a shove of his backside ; and puts* AYAMONN *to the other end of the room with a push on the shoulder.*

33

BRENNAN

(*as he pushes* SHEILA)

Outa th' way, there ! Stem your eagerness for
a second, will yous ? All in good time. Give the
man a chance to get himself easy. (*As he pushes*
AYAMONN) Farther back, there, farther back !
Give th' performer a chance to dispose himself.
Isn't he a swell, wha' ? The centre group's to be
dhressed the same way, while th' corner men'll
be in reverse colours — green coats, black trousers,
an' white vest, see ? Th' whole assembly'll look
famous. Benjamin's lendin' all the set o' twelve
suits for five bob, 'cause o' th' reason we're runnin'
th' Show for. (*To* SHEILA — *in a hoarse whisper*)
You stare at the fire as if he wasn't here. He's
extravagant in shyness, an' sinks away into con-
fusion at the stare of an eye — understand ?

> [*She slowly, and a little sullenly, sits down to
> stare into the fire. The door is opened,
> and in comes* ROORY O'BALACAUN *with a
> small roll of Irish Magazines under an
> arm. He is a stout middle-aged man,
> dressed in rough homespun coat, cap, and
> knee-breeches, wearing over all a trench coat.*

ROORY

Here y'are, Ayamonn, me son, avic's th' Irish
magazines I got me friend to pinch for you. (*He
looks at the* SINGER.) Hello, what kind of a circus is
it's goin' on here ?

AYAMONN

Mr. Brennan Moore here's organising the singers

34

for the Minsthrel Show to help get funds in case we have to go on sthrike, Roory.

ROORY

I'm one o' th' men meself, but I don't stand for a foreign Minsthrel Show bein' held, an' the Sword of Light gettin' lifted up in th' land. We want no coon or Kaffir industry in our country.

BRENNAN
(*indignantly*)

Doesn't matter what you stand for before you came here, you'll sit down now. Thry to regard yourself as a civilised member of the community, man, an' hold your peace for th' present. (*To the* SINGER) Now, Sam, me son o' gold, excavate the shyness out of your system an' sing as if you were performin' before a Royal Command!

ROORY
(*with a growl*)

There's no royal commands wanted here.

BRENNAN
(*with a gesture of disgusted annoyance*)

Will you for goodness' sake not be puttin' th' singer out? I used the term only as an allegory, man.

ROORY

Allegory man, or allegory woman, there's goin' to be no royal inthrusions where the Sword o' Light is shinin'.

AYAMONN

Aw, for Christ's sake, Roory, let's hear the song !

BRENNAN

(*to the* SINGER, *who has been coughing shyly and turning sideways from his audience*)

Now, Sam, remember you're not in your working clothes, an' are a different man, entirely. Chin up and chest out. (*He gives a note or two on the melodeon.*) Now !

SINGER

(*singing*)

A sober black shawl hides her body entirely,
Touch'd by th' sun and th' salt spray of the
    sea ;
But down in th' darkness a slim hand, so
    lovely,
Carries a rich bunch of red roses for me.
   [*He turns away a little more from his audience,
    and coughs shyly.*

BRENNAN

(*enthusiastically*)

Sam, you're excellin' yourself ! On again, me oul' son !

SINGER

(*singing*)

Her petticoat's simple, her feet are but bare,
An' all that she has is but neat an' scantie ;
But stars in th' deeps of her eyes are
    exclaiming
I carry a rich bunch of red roses for thee !

36

(*after giving a few curling notes on the melodeon*)
A second Count McCormack in th' makin' ! An'
whenever he sung Mother Mo Chree, wasn't
there a fewroory in Heaven with the rush that
was made to lean over an' hear him singin' it !

[*While* BRENNAN *has been speaking, the door
has opened, and* MULLCANNY *now stands
there gaping into the room. He is young,
lusty, and restless. He is wearing fine
tweeds that don't fit too well ; and his tweed
cap is set rakishly on his head. He, too,
wears a mackintosh.*

MULLCANNY

Is this a home-sweet-away-from-home hippo-
dhrome, or what ?

BRENNAN
(*clicking his tongue in annoyance*)
Dtchdtchdtch !

MULLCANNY

An' did I hear someone pratin' about Heaven,
an' I coming in ? (*To* BRENNAN — *tapping him
on the shoulder*) Haven't you heard, old man, that
God is dead ?

BRENNAN

Well, keep your grand discovery to yourself for a
minute or two more, please. (*To the* SINGER)
Now, Sam, apologisin' for th' other's rudeness,
the last verse, please.

37

SINGER
(*singing*)

No arrogant gem sits enthron'd on her fore-
head,
Or swings from a white ear for all men to see;
But jewel'd desire in a bosom, most pearly,
Carries a rich bunch of red roses for me!

BRENNAN
(*after another curl of notes on the melodeon*)
Well, fair damsel and gentlemen all, what do you
think of the song and the singer?

AYAMONN
The song was good, and the singer was splendid.

MULLCANNY
What I heard of it wasn't bad.

SINGER
(*shyly*)
I'm glad I pleased yous all.

RORY
(*dubiously*)
D'ye not think th' song is a trifle indecent?

MULLCANNY
(*mockingly*)
Indecent! And what may your eminence's
specification of indecency be? (*Angrily*) Are
you catalogued, too, with the Catholic Young

38

Men going about with noses long as a snipe's bill, sthripping the gayest rose of its petals in search of a beetle, and sniffing a taint in the freshest breeze blowing in from the sea ?

BRENNAN
(*warningly*)
Lady present, lady present, boys !

ROORY
It ill becomes a thrue Gael to stand unruffled when either song or story thries to introduce colour to the sabler nature of yearnin's in un-tuthored minds.

BRENNAN
(*more loudly*)
Lady present, boys !

SHEILA
(*rising out of the chair and going towards the door*)
The lady's going now, thank you all for the entertainment. (*To* AYAMONN) I won't stay any longer to disturb the important dispute of your friends.

AYAMONN
(*going over to her*)
Don't be foolish, Sheila, dear ; but if you must go, you must. We'll see each other again tomorrow evening.

SHEILA
(*firmly*)
No, not tomorrow, nor the next night either.

39

AYAMONN

(*while* BRENNAN *plays softly on the melodeon to
hide embarrassment*)

When then ?

SHEILA

I can't tell. I'll write. Never maybe. (*Bitterly*)
I warned you this night might be the last chance
of a talk for some time, and you didn't try to
make use of it !

AYAMONN

(*catching her arm*)

I made as much use of it as you'd let me.
Tomorrow night, in the old place, near the bridge,
the bridge of vision where we first saw Aengus
and his coloured birds of passion passing.

SHEILA

(*wildly*)

I can't ; I won't, so there — oh, let me go !
[*She breaks away from him, runs out, and a
silence falls on the room for a few moments.*

ROORY

(*breaking the silence*)

Women is strange things ! Elegant animals, not
knowin' their own minds a minute.

BRENNAN

(*consolingly*)

She'll come back, she'll come back.

AYAMONN

(*trying to appear unconcerned*)

Aw, to hell with her !

40

SINGER
(*faintly*)
Can I go now ?

BRENNAN
Wait, an' I'll be with you in a second.

MULLCANNY
(*to* AYAMONN)
I just dropped in to say, Ayamonn, that I'll be getting Haeckel's *Riddle of the Universe* tomorrow, afther long searching, and I'll let you have it the minute it comes into my hand.

[*The door is suddenly flung wide open, and* EEADA, *followed by* DYMPNA *and* FINNOOLA, *with others, mingled with men behind them, rushes into the room in a very excited state. She comes forward, with her two companions a little behind, while the rest group themselves by the door.*

EEADA
(*distractedly*)
It's gone she is, an' left us lonesome ; vanished she is like a fairy mist of an early summer mornin' ; stolen she is be some pagan Protestan' hand, envious of the love we had for our sweet Lady of Eblana's poor !

AYAMONN
Nonsense ; no Protestant hand touched her. Where was she ?

Safe in her niche in th' hall she was, afther her
washin', lookin' down on the comin's an' goin's
of her strugglin' children : an' then we missed
her, an' th' niche was empty !

THE REST
(*in chorus*)
An' dear knows what woe'll fall on our poor
house now.

BRENNAN
An' a good job, too. (*Passionately*) Inflamin'
yourselves with idols that have eyes an' see not ;
ears, an' hear not ; an' have hands that handle
not ; like th' chosen people setting' moon-images
an' sun-images, cuttin' away the thrue and
homely connection between the Christian an' his
God ! Here, let me and me singer out of this
unholy place !
[*He pushes his way through the people,
followed by the* SINGER, *and goes out.*

EEADA
(*nodding her head, to* AYAMONN)
All bark, but no bite ! We know him of old : a
decent oul' blatherer. Sure, doesn't he often buy
violets and snowdhrops, even, for little Ursula,
below, tellin' her she mustn't put them before a
graven image, knowin' full well that that was th'
first thing she'd hurry home to do. An' she's
breakin' her young heart below, now, because her
dear Lady has left her. (*Suspiciously*) If oul'

Brennan had a hand in her removal, woe betide him.

MULLCANNY
(*mocking*)
Couldn't you all do bether than wasting your time making gods afther your own ignorant images?

AYAMONN
(*silencing him with a gesture*)
That's enough, Paudhrig. (*To* EEADA) Tell little Ursula not to worry. Her Lady'll come back. If your Lady of Eblana hasn't returned by tonight, I'll surrender my sleep afther my night's work to search for her, and bring her back safe to her niche in the hall. No one in this house touched Her.

EADA
An' you'll see She'll pay you back for your kindness, Ayamonn — (*looking at* MULLCANNY) — though it's little surprised I'd be if, of her own accord, She came down indignant, an' slipped off from us, hearin' the horrid talk that's allowed to float around this house lately.

MULLCANNY
(*mocking*)
Afraid of me, She was. Well, Ayamonn, I've some lessons to get ready, so I'll be off. I'll bring you the book tomorrow. (*To the crowd — mocking*) Ihope the poor Lady of Eblana's poor'll find her way home again.
[*He goes out through a surly-faced crowd.*

43

AYAMONN
(*to* EEADA)

Don't mind Mullcanny. Good night, now ; and don't worry about your dear statue. If She doesn't come back, we'll find another as bright and good to take her place.

EEADA
(*growling*)

The fella that's gone'll have a rough end, jeerin' things sacred to our feelin'. For his own sake, I hope th' B. Virgin'll come to live with us all again.

[*They all go out, and* AYAMONN *is left alone with* ROORY. AYAMONN *takes off his doublet, folds it up, and puts it back in the basket. He goes into the other room and comes back with oilskin coat and thigh-high leggings. He puts the leggings on over his trousers.*

AYAMONN
(*putting on the leggings*)

Th' shunting-yard'll be a nice place to be tonight. D'ye hear it ? (*He listens to the falling rain, now heavier than ever.*)

ROORY

Fallin' fast. That Mullcanny'll get into throuble yet.

AYAMONN

Not he. He's really a good fellow. Gave up his job rather than his beliefs — more'n many would do.

ROORY

An' how does he manage now ?

44

AYAMONN

Hammering knowledge into deluded minds wishing to be civil servants, bank clerks, an' constables who hope to take the last sacraments as sergeants in the Royal Irish Constabulary or the Metropolitan Police.

ROORY

By God, he's his work cut out for him with the last lot !

[*The door is again opened and* EEADA *sticks her head into the room.*

EEADA

Your mother's just sent word that the woman she's mindin's bad, an' she'll have to stay th' night. I'm just runnin' round meself to make your mother a cup o' tea.

AYAMONN
(*irritably*)

Dtch dtch — she'll knock herself up before she's done ! When I lock up, I'll leave the key with you for her, Eeada. (*He lights a shunter's lantern and puts out the lamp.*)

EEADA

Right y'are.   [*She goes.*

ROORY

What kid was it sketched th' angel on th' wall ?

AYAMONN

Oh, I did that. I'd give anything to be a painter.

45

ROORY

What, like Oul' Brennan on th' Moor ?

AYAMONN

No, no ; like Angelico or Constable.

ROORY
(*indifferently*)
Never heard of them.

AYAMONN
(*musingly*)
To throw a whole world in colour on a canvas
though it be but a man's fine face, a woman's
shape asthride of a cushioned couch, or a three-
bordered house on a hill, done with a glory ; even
delaying God, busy forgin' a new world, to stay
awhile an' look upon their loveliness.

ROORY

Aw, Ayamonn, Ayamonn, man, put out your
hand an' see if you're awake ! (*He fiddles with
the books on the table.*)   What oul' book are you
readin' now ?

AYAMONN
(*dressed now in oilskin leggings and coat, with
an oilskin sou'wester on his head, comes over
to look at the book in* ROORY's *hand, and shines
the lantern on it*)
Oh, that's Ruskin's *Crown of Wild Olives* — a
grand book — I'll lend it to you.

ROORY

What for ?   What would I be doin' with it ?   I've

46

no time to waste on books. Ruskin. Curious
name ; not Irish, is it ?

AYAMONN

No, a Scotsman who wrote splendidly about a lot
of things. Listen to this, spoken before a gathering
of business men about to build an Exchange in
their town.

ROORY

Aw, Ayamonn — an Exchange ! What have we
got to do with an Exchange ?

AYAMONN
(impatiently)

Listen a second, man ! Ruskin, speakin' to the
business men, says : " Your ideal of life is a
pleasant and undulating world, with iron and coal
everywhere beneath it. On each pleasant bank
of this world is to be a beautiful mansion ; stables,
and coach - houses ; a park and hot - houses ;
carriage-drives and shrubberies ; and here are to
live the votaries of the Goddess of Getting-On —
the English gentleman——"

ROORY
(interrupting)

There you are, you see, Ayamonn — th' English
gentleman !

AYAMONN

Wait a second — Irish or English — a gentleman's th' same.

ROORY

'Tisn't. I'm tellin' you it's different. What's in

47

this Ruskin of yours but another oul' cod with a
gift of the gab ?   Right enough for th' English,
pinin' afther little things, ever rakin' cindhers for
th' glint o' gold.   We're different — we have th'
light.

AYAMONN
You mean th' Catholic Faith ?

ROORY
(*impatiently*)
No, no ; that's there, too ; I mean th' light of
freedom ; th' tall white candle tipped with its
golden spear of flame.   The light we thought we'd
lost ; but it burns again, sthrengthenin' into a
sword of light.   Like in th' song we sung together
th' other night.   (*He sings softly.*)

Our courage so many have thought to be
    agein',
Now flames like a brilliant new star in th' sky;
And Danger is proud to be call'd a good
    brother,
For Freedom has buckled her sword on her
    thigh.

AYAMONN
(*joining in*)
Then out to th' place where th' battle is bravest,
Where th' noblest an' meanest fight fierce in
    th' fray,
There Republican banners shall mock at th'
    foemen,
An' Fenians shall turn th' dark night into day !
48

[*A pause as the two of them stand silent, each clasping the other's hand.* AYAMONN *opens the door to pass out.*

ROORY
(*in a tense whisper*)
Th' Fenians are in force again, Ayamonn ; th'
Sword o' Light is shinin' !
[*They go out, and* AYAMONN *closes the door as the Curtain falls.*

ACT II

SCENE : *The same as in Act I.*

It is about ten o'clock at night. The rain has stopped, and there is a fine moon sailing through the sky. Some of its rays come in through the window at the side.

AYAMONN, *in his shirt-sleeves, is sitting at the table. He has an ordinary tin money-box in his hand, and a small pile of coppers, mixed with a few sixpences, are on the table beside him. He is just taking the last coin from the slit in the box with the aid of a knife-blade. His mother is by the dresser piling up the few pieces of crockery used for a recent meal. The old one-wick lamp is alight, and stands on the table near to AYAMONN. Several books lie open there, too.*

AYAMONN

There's th' last one out, now. It's quite a job getting them out with a knife.

MRS. BREYDON

Why don't you put them in a box with a simple lid on ?

AYAMONN

The harder it is to get at, the less chance of me spending it on something more necessary than what I seek. (*He counts the money on the table.*) One bob — two — three — an' sixpence — an'

50

nine — three an' ninepence ; one an' threepence
to get yet — a long way to go.

MRS. BREYDON

Maybe, now, th' bookseller would give you it for
what you have till you can give him th' rest.

AYAMONN

(*in agony*)

Aw, woman, if you can't say sense, say nothing !
Constable's reproductions are five shillings second-
hand, an' he that's selling is the bastard that nearly
got me jailed for running off with his Shakespeare.
It's touch an go if he'll let me have it for the five
bob.

MRS. BREYDON

(*philosophically*)

Well, seein' you done without it so long, you can
go without it longer.

AYAMONN

(*with firm conviction*)

I'll have it the first week we get the extra shilling
the men are demandin'.

MRS. BREYDON

I shouldn't count your chickens before they're
hatched.

AYAMONN

(*joking a little bitterly*)

Perhaps our blessed Lady of Eblana's poor will
work a miracle for me.

MRS. BREYDON
(*a little anxiously*)

Hush, don't say that! Jokin' or serious, Ayamonn, I wouldn't say that. We don't believe
in any of their Blessed Ladies, but as it's somethin' sacred, it's best not mentioned. (*She
shuffles into her shawl.*) Though it's a queer
thing, Her goin' off out of Her niche without a
one in th' house knowin' why. They're all out
huntin' for Her still.

> The door opens, and BRENNAN *comes in
> slowly, with a cute grin on his face. He
> has a large package, covered with paper,
> under an arm.*

BRENNAN

Out huntin' still for Her they are, are they?
Well, let them hunt; she's here! A prisoner
under me arm!

MRS. BREYDON
(*indignantly*)

Well, Mr. Brennan Moore, it's ashamed of yourself you should be yokin' th' poor people to
throubled anxiety over their treasure; and little
Ursula breakin' her heart into th' bargain.

AYAMONN

It's god-damned mean of you, Brennan! What
good d'ye think you'll do by this rowdy love of
your own opinions — forcing tumult into the
minds of ignorant, anxious people?

52

BRENNAN
(*calmly*)

Wait till yous see, wait till yous see, before yous
are sorry for sayin' more.

[*He removes the paper and shows the lost
image transfigured into a figure looking as
if it had come straight from the shop : the
white dress is spotless, the blue robe radiant,
and the gold along its border and on the
crown is gleaming. He holds it up for
admiration.*

BRENNAN
(*triumphantly*)

There, what d'ye think of Her now ? Fair as th'
first grand tinge of th' dawn, She is, an' bright as
th' star of the evenin'.

MRS. BREYDON

Glory be to God, isn't She lovely ! But hurry
Her off, Brennan, for She's not a thing for
Protestant eyes to favour.

AYAMONN
(*a little testily*)

Put it back, Brennan, put it back, and don't
touch it again.

BRENNAN

Isn't that what I'm goin' to do ? Oh, boy alive,
won't they get th' shock o' their lives when they
see Her shinin' in th' oul' spot. (*He becomes
serious.*) Though, mind you, me thrue mind
misgives me for decoratin' what's a charm to the

people of Judah in th' worship of idols ; but th'
two of you is witness I did it for the sake of the
little one, and not in any tilt towards honour to a
graven image.

MRS. BREYDON
(*resignedly*)

It's done now, God forgive us both, an' me for
sayin' She's lovely. Touchin' a thing forbidden
with a startled stir of praise !

AYAMONN

Put it back, put it back, man, and leave it quiet
where you got it first.

[BRENNAN *goes out, looking intently out, and
listening, before he does so.*

MRS. BREYDON

He meant well, poor man, but he's done a
dangerous thing. I'll be back before you start
for work. (*With a heavy sigh.*) It won't take us
long to tend her for the last time. The white
sheets have come, th' tall candles wait to be lit,
an' th' coffin's ordhered, an' th' room'll look
sacred with the bunch of violets near her head.
(*She goes out slowly — as she goes*) Dear knows
what'll happen to th' three childhren.

[AYAMONN *sits silent for a few moments,
reading a book, his elbows resting on the
table.*

AYAMONN
(*with a deep sigh — murmuringly*)

Sheila, Sheila, my heart cries out for you ! (*After
a moment's pause, he reads.*)

54

But I am pigeon-livered, an' lack gall
To make oppression bitther ; or, ere this,
I should have fatted all th' region kites
With this slave's offal : Bloody, bawdy villain !
Oh, Will, you were a boyo ; a brave boyo, though,
and a beautiful one !

[*The door opens and* OLD BRENNAN *comes in,
showing by his half-suppressed chuckles
that he is enjoying himself. He wanders
over the room to stand by the fire.*

BRENNAN
(*chuckling*)
In Her old place she is, now, in Her new corona-
tion robe ; and funny it is to think it's the last
place they'll look for Her.

AYAMONN
I'm busy, now.

BRENNAN
(*sitting down by the fire*)
Ay, so you are ; so I see ; busy readin'. Read
away, for I won't disturb you ; only have a few
quiet puffs at th' oul' pipe. (*A pause.*) Ah, then,
don't I wish I was young enough to bury meself
in th' joy of readin' all th' great books of th'
world. Ah ! but when I was young, I had to
work hard.

AYAMONN
I work hard, too.

BRENNAN
Course you do ! Isn't that what I'm sayin' ?

An' all th' more credit, too, though it must be thryin' to have thoughtless people comin' in an' intherferin' with the golden movements of your thoughts.

AYAMONN

It's often a damned nuisance!

BRENNAN

'Course it is. Isn't that what I'm sayin'? (*As the door opens*) An' here's another o' th' boobies entherin' now. (ROORY *comes in, and shuts the door rather noisily.*) Eh, go easy, there — can't you see Ayamonn's busy studyin'?

ROORY

(*coming and bending over* AYAMONN)

Are you still lettin' oul' Ruskin tease you?

AYAMONN

(*angrily*)

No, no; Shakespeare, Shakespeare, this time! (*Springing from his chair*) Damn it, can't you let a man alone a minute? What th' hell d'ye want now?

BRENNAN

(*warningly*)

I told you he was busy.

ROORY

(*apologetically*)

Aw, I only came with the tickets you asked me to bring you for the comin' National Anniversary of Terence Bellew MacManus.

AYAMONN

All right, all right ; let's have them.

ROORY

How many d'ye want ?   How many can you sell ?

AYAMONN

Give me twelve sixpennies ; if the sthrike doesn't
come off I'll easily sell that number.

ROORY

(*counting out the tickets which* AYAMONN *gathers
up and puts into his pocket*)
I met that Mullcanny on the way with a book
for you ; but he stopped to tell a couple of railwaymen that the story of Adam an' Eve was all a cod.

BRENNAN

(*indignantly*)
He has a lot o' the people here in a state o'
steamin' anger, goin' about with his bitther belief
that the patthern of a man's hand is nearly at
one with a monkey's paw, a horse's foot, th'
flipper of a seal, or th' wing of a bat !

AYAMONN

Well, each of them is as wonderful as the hand
of a man.

ROORY

No, Ayamonn, not from the Christian point of
view.   D'ye know what they're callin' him round
here ?   Th' New Broom, because he's always
sayin' he'll sweep th' idea of God clean outa th'
mind o' man.

BRENNAN

(*excited*)

There'll be dire damage done to him yet! He was goin' to be flattened out be a docker th' other day for tellin' him that a man first formin' showed an undoubted sign of a tail.

AYAMONN

Ay, and when he's fully formed, if he doesn't show the tail, he shows most signs of all that goes along with it.

ROORY

But isn't that a nice dignity to put on th' sacredness of a man's conception!

BRENNAN

(*whisperingly*)

An' a lot o' them are sayin', Ayamonn, that your encouragement of him should come to an end.

AYAMONN

Indeed? Well, let them. I'll stand by any honest man seekin' th' truth, though his way isn't my way. (*To* BRENNAN) You, yourself, go about deriding many things beloved by your Catholic neighbours.

BRENNAN

I contest only dangerous deceits specified be the Council o' Thrent, that are nowhere scheduled in th' pages of the Holy Scriptures.

ROORY

Yes, Ayamonn, it's altogether different; he just

goes about blatherin' in his ignorant Protestant way.

BRENNAN
(*highly indignant*)
Ignorant, am I ? An' where would a body find an ignorance lustier than your own, eh ? If your Council o' Thrent's ordher for prayers for the dead who are past help, your dismal veneration of Saints an' Angels, your images of wood an' stone, carved an' coloured, have given you the image an' superscription of a tail, th' pure milk of the gospel has made a man of me, Godfearin', but stately, with a mind garlanded to th' steady an' eternal thruth !

[*While they have been arguing*, MULLCANNY *has peeped round the door, and now comes into the room, eyeing the two disputants with a lot of amusement and a little scorn. They take no notice of him.*

ROORY
Sure, man, you have the neighbourhood hectored with your animosity against Catholic custom an' Catholic thought, never hesitatin' to give th' Pope even a deleterious name.

BRENNAN
(*lapsing, in his excitement, into a semi-Ulster dialect*)
We dud ut tae yeh in Durry, on' sent your bravest floatin' down dud in th' wathers of th' Boyne, like th' hosts of Pharaoh tumblin' in the rush of

59

th' Rud Sea ! Thut was a slup in th' puss tae your Pope !

MULLCANNY

You pair of damned fools, don't you know that the Pope wanted King Billy to win, and that the Vatican was ablaze with lights of joy afther King James's defeat over the wathers of the Boyne ?

ROORY

You're a liar, he didn't !

BRENNAN

You're a liar, it wasn't !
[*They turn from* MULLCANNY *to continue the row with themselves.*

BRENNAN

Looksee, if I believed in the ministhration of Saints on' Angels, I'd say thut th' good Protestant St. Puthrick was at the hud of what fell out at Durry, Aughrim, on' th' Boyne.

ROORY

(*stunned with the thought of St. Patrick as a Protestant*)

Protestant St. Pathrick ? Is me hearin' sound, or what ? What name did you mention ?

BRENNAN

I said St. Puthrick — th' evangelical founder of our thrue Church.

ROORY

Is it dhreamin' I am ? Is somethin' happenin'

60

to me, or is it happenin' to you? Oh, man, it's mixin' mirth with madness you are at thinkin' St. Pathrick ever looped his neck in an orange sash, or tapped out a tune on a Protestant dhrum! Let us only keep silent for a minute or two, an' we'll hear him sayin' that th' hymn St. Pathrick sung an' he on th' way to meet King Laeghaire, an' quench th' fire o' Tara, was Lilly Bullero Bullen a Law!

BRENNAN
(*contemptuously*)

I refuse to argue with a one who's no' a broad-minded mon. Abuse is no equivalent for lugic — so I say God save th' King, an' tae hull with th' Pope!

ROORY
(*indignantly*)

You damned bigot — to hell with th' King, an' God save th' Pope!

MULLCANNY
(*To* AYAMONN)

You see how they live in bittherness, the one with the other. Envy, strife, and malice crawl from the coloured slime of the fairy-tales that go to make what is called religion. (*Taking a book from his pocket*) Here's something can bear a thousand tests, showing neatly how the world and all it bears upon it came into slow existence over millions of years, doing away for ever with the funny wonders of the seven days' creation set out in the fairy book of the Bible.

AYAMONN

(*taking the book from* MULLCANNY)

Thanks, Pether, oul' son ; I'm bound to have a good time reading it.

MULLCANNY

It'll give you the true and scientific history of man as he was before Adam.

BRENNAN

(*in a woeful voice*)

It's a darkened mind that thries tae lower us to what we were before th' great an' good God fashioned us. What does ony sensible person want to know what we were like before the creation of th' first man ?

AYAMONN

(*murmuringly*)

To know the truth, to seek the truth, is good, though it lead to th' danger of eternal death.

ROORY

(*horror-stricken — crossing himself*)

Th' Lord between us an' all harm !

BRENNAN

(*whispering prayerfully*)

Lord, I believe, help Thou mine unbelief.

MULLCANNY

(*pointing out a picture in the book*)

See ? The human form unborn. The tail — look ; the os coccyx sticking a mile out ; there's no getting away from it !

BRENNAN

(*shaking his head woefully*)

An' this is holy Ireland!

ROORY

(*lifting his eyes to the ceiling — woefully*)

Poor St. Pathrick!

MULLCANNY

(*mockingly*)

He's going to be a lonely man soon, eh? (*To* AYAMONN) Keep it safe for me, Ayamonn. When you've read it, you'll be a different man. (*He goes to the door.*) Well, health with the whole o' you, and goodbye for the present.　　　[*He goes out.*

ROORY

Have nothin' to do with that book, Ayamonn, for that fellow gone out would rip up the floor of Heaven to see what was beneath it. It's clapped in jail he ought to be!

BRENNAN

An' th' book banned!

AYAMONN

Roory, Roory, is that th' sort o' freedom you'd bring to Ireland with a crowd of green branches an' th' joy of shouting? If we give no room to men of our time to question many things, all things, ay, life itself, then freedom's but a paper flower, a star of tinsel, a dead lass with gay ribbons at her breast an' a gold comb in her hair.

63

Let us bring freedom here, not with sounding brass an' tinkling cymbal, but with silver trumpets blowing, with a song all men can sing, with a palm branch in our hand, rather than with a whip at our belt, and a headsman's axe on our shoulders.

[*There is a gentle knock at the door, and the voice of* SHEILA *is heard speaking.*

SHEILA
(*outside*)
Ayamonn, are you there ?   Are you in ?

BRENNAN
(*whispering*)
The little lass ;   I knew she'd come back.

AYAMONN
I don't want her to see you here.   Go into the other room — quick. (*He pushes them towards it.*)   An' keep still.

ROORY
(*To* BRENNAN)
An' don't you go mockin' our Pope, see ?

BRENNAN
(*To* ROORY)
Nor you go singlin' out King Billy for a jeer.

AYAMONN
In with yous, quick !

BRENNAN
I prophesied she'd come back, didn't I, Ayamonn? that she'd come back, didn't I ?

64

AYAMONN

Yes, yes ; in you go.

[*He puts them in the other room and shuts
the door.   Then he crosses the room and
opens the door to admit* SHEILA.   *She comes
in, and he and* SHEILA *stand silently for
some moments, she trying to look at him,
and finding it hard.*

SHEILA
(*at last*)

Well, haven't you anything to say to me ?

AYAMONN
(*slowly and coldly*)

I waited for you at the bridge today ; but you
didn't come.

SHEILA

I couldn't come ; I told you why.

AYAMONN

I was very lonely.

SHEILA
(*softly*)

So was I, Ayamonn, lonely even in front of God's
holy face.

AYAMONN

Sheila, we've gone a long way in a gold canoe,
over many waters, bright and surly, sometimes
sending bitter spray asplash on our faces, forcing
forward to the green glade of united work and
united rest beyond the farther waves.   But you
were ever listening for the beat from the wings

65

of the angel of fear. So you got out to walk safe
on a crowded road.

This is a cold and cheerless welcome, Ayamonn.

AYAMONN

Change, if you want to, the burning kiss falling
on the upturned, begging mouth for the chill
caress of a bony, bearded Saint. (*Loudly*) Go
with th' yelling crowd, and keep them brave, and
yell along with them !

SHEILA

Won't you listen, then, to the few words I have
to say ?

AYAMONN

(*sitting down near the fire, and looking into it,
        though he leaves her standing*)
Go ahead ; I won't fail to hear you.

SHEILA

God knows I don't mean to hurt you, but you
must know that we couldn't begin to live on what
you're earning now — could we ? (*He keeps
silent.*) Oh, Ayamonn, why do you waste your
time on doing foolish things ?

AYAMONN

What foolish things ?
[*A hubbub is heard in the street outside ;
    voices saying loudly " Give him one in the
    bake " or " Down him with a one in th'*
66

*belly"; then the sound of running foot-
steps, and silence.*

SHEILA

(*when she hears the voices — nervously*)
What's that?

AYAMONN

(*without taking his gaze from the fire*)
Some drunken row or other.
          [*They listen silently for a few moments.*

AYAMONN

Well, what foolish things?

SHEILA

(*timid and hesitating*)
You know yourself, Ayamonn: trying to paint,
going mad about Shakespeare, and consorting
with a kind of people that can only do you harm.

AYAMONN

(*mockingly prayerful — raising his eyes to the
ceiling*)
O Lord, let me forsake the foolish, and live; and
go in the way of Sheila's understanding!

SHEILA

(*going over nearer to him*)
Listen, Ayamonn, my love; you know what I
say is only for our own good, that we may come
together all the sooner. (*Trying to speak jokingly*)
Now, really, isn't it comical I'd look if I were to
go about in a scanty petticoat, covered in a sober

black shawl, and my poor feet bare. (*Mocking*)
Wouldn't I look well that way !

AYAMONN
(*quietly*)
With red roses in your hand, you'd look beautiful.

SHEILA
(*desperately*)
Oh, for goodness' sake, Ayamonn, be sensible !
I'm getting a little tired of all this. I can't bear
the strain the way we're going on much longer.
(*A short pause.*) You will either have to make
good, or—— (*She pauses.*)

AYAMONN
(*quietly*)
Or what ?

SHEILA
(*with a little catch in her voice*)
Or lose me ; and you wouldn't like that to happen.

AYAMONN
I shouldn't like that to happen ; but I could bear
the sthrain.

SHEILA
I risked a big row tonight to come to tell you
good news : I've been told that the strike is bound
to take place ; there is bound to be trouble ; and,
if you divide yourself from the foolish men, and
stick to your job, you'll soon be a foreman of
some kind or other.

AYAMONN

(*rising from his seat and facing her for the first time*)

Who told you all this ?   The Inspector ?

SHEILA

Never mind who ; if he did, wasn't it decent of him ?

AYAMONN

D'ye know what you're asking me to do, woman ? To be a blackleg ; to blast with th' black frost of desertion the gay hopes of my comrades. Whatever you may think them to be, they are my comrades. Whatever they may say or do, they remain my brothers and sisters. Go to hell, girl, I have a soul to save as well as you. (*With a catch in his voice*) Oh, Sheila, you shouldn't have asked me to do this thing !

SHEILA

(*trying to come close, but he pushes her back*)

Oh, Ayamonn, it is a chance ; take it, do, for my sake !

[*Rapid footsteps are heard outside. The door flies open and* MULLCANNY *comes in, pale, frightened, his clothes dishevelled, and a slight smear of blood on his forehead. His bowler hat is crushed down on his head, his coat is torn, and his waistcoat unbuttoned, showing his tie pulled out of its place. He sinks into a chair.*

AYAMONN

What's happened ?   Who did that to you ?

MULLCANNY

Give's a drink, someone, will you ?
> [AYAMONN *gets him a drink from a jug on the dresser.*

MULLCANNY

A gang of bowseys made for me, and I talking to a man.   Barely escaped with my life.   Weekly communicants, probably, the scoundrels !   Only for some brave oul' one, they'd have laid me out completely.   She saved me from worse.

AYAMONN

How th' hell did you bring all that on you ?

MULLCANNY
(*plaintively*)

Just trying to show a fellow the foolishness of faith in a hereafter, when something struck me on the head, and I was surrounded by feet making kicks at me !
> [*A crash of breaking glass is heard from the other room, and* BRENNAN *and* ROORY *come running out of it.*

ROORY

A stone has done for th' window !   (*He sees* MULLCANNY.)   Oh, that's how th' land lies, is it ? Haven't I often said that if you go round leerin' at God an' His holy assistants, one day He's bound to have a rap at you !

70

BRENNAN

Keep away from that window, there, in case another one comes sailin' in.

> [*Immediately he has spoken, a stone smashes in through the window.* BRENNAN *lies down flat on the floor ;* MULLCANNY *slides from the chair and crouches on the ground ;* ROORY *gets down on his hands and knees, keeping his head as low as possible, so that he resembles a Mohammedan at his devotions ;* SHEILA *stands stiff in a corner, near the door ; and* AYAMONN, *seizing up a hurley lying against the dresser, makes for the door to go out.*

BRENNAN

I guessed this was comin'.

AYAMONN
(angrily)

I'll show them !

SHEILA
(*To* AYAMONN)

Stop where you are, you fool !

> [*But* AYAMONN *pays no attention to the advice and hurries out of the door.*

ROORY
(plaintively and with dignity — to MULLCANNY)

This is what you bring down on innocent people, trimmed into a sane outlook on life with your obstinate association of man with th' lower animals.

71

MULLCANNY

(*truculently*)

Only created impudence it is that strives to set yourselves above the ape's formation, genetically present in every person's body.

BRENNAN

(*indignantly*)

String out life to where it started, an' you'll find no sign, let alone a proof, of the dignity, wisdom, an' civility of man ever having been associated with th' manners of a monkey.

MULLCANNY

And why do children like to climb trees, eh? Answer me that?

ROORY

(*fiercely*)

They love it more where you come from than they do here. Here's one wouldn't be surprised to hear that waggin' tails followed all who jumped about th' waste o' wild Killorglan!

SHEILA

(*from her corner*)

It's surely to be pitied you are, young man, lettin' yourself be bullied by ignorant books into believing that things are naught but what poor men are inclined to call them, blind to the glorious and eternal facts that shine behind them.

MULLCANNY

(*pityingly*)

Bullied be books — eternal facts — aw! Yous

are all scared stiff at the manifestation of a truth or two. D'ye know that the contraction of catharrh, apoplexy, consumption, and cataract of the eye is common to the monkeys ? Knowledge you have now that you hadn't before ; and a lot of them even like beer.

ROORY

Well, that's something sensible, at last.

BRENNAN
(*fiercely*)

Did they get their likin' for beer from us, or did we get our likin' of beer from them ? Answer me that, you, now ; answer me that !

ROORY

Answer him that. We're not Terra Del Fooay-geeans, but sensible, sane, an' civilised souls.

MULLCANNY
(*gleefully*)

Time's promoted reptiles — that's all ; yous can't do away with the os coccyges !

BRENNAN

Ladies present, ladies present.

ROORY
(*creeping over rapidly till his face is close to
that of* MULLCANNY'*s* — *fiercely*)

We can get away from you, despoiler of words comin' from th' mouth of men ! We stand on the

earth, firm, upright, heads cocked, lookin' all men
in th' face, afraid o' nothin' ; men o' goodwill
we are, abloom with th' blessin' o' charity,
showin' in th' dust we're made of, th' diamond-
core of an everlastin' divinity !

SHEILA
(*excitedly*)
Hung as high as Guilderoy he ought to be, an' he
deep in the evil of his rich illusions, spouting
insults at war with th' mysteries an' facts of our
holy faith !

BRENNAN
(*to* SHEILA)
Hush, pretty lady, hush. (*To the others*) Boys,
boys, take example from a poor oul' Protestant
here, never lettin' himself be offended be a quiver
of anger in any peaceable or terrified discussion.
Now, let that last word finish it ; finis — the end,
see ?

ROORY
(*angrily — to* BRENNAN)
Finis yousself, you blurry-eyed, wither-skinned
oul' greybeard, singin' songs in th' public streets
for odd coppers, with all th' boys in th' Bank of
Ireland workin' overtime countin' all you've got
in their front room ! Finis you !

BRENNAN
(*indignantly*)
Bleatin' perjury out of you, y'are, about my
possession of a few coins an office-boy, in a hurry,
wouldn't stop to pick up from th' path before

74

him ! An' as for withered, soople as you I am, hands that can tinkle a thremblin' tune out of an oul' melodeon, legs that can carry me ten miles an' more, an' eyes that can still see without hardship a red berry shinin' from a distant bush !

[*The door opens and* AYAMONN *and his mother come in. She runs over to the blossoms at the window, tenderly examining the plants growing there — the musk, geranium, and the fuchsia.*

MRS. BREYDON
(*joyfully*)

Unharmed, th' whole of them. Th' stone passed them by, touchin' none o' them — thank God for that mercy !

AYAMONN

What th' hell are you doin' on your knees ? Get up, get up. (*They rise from the floor shamefacedly.*) Th' rioters all dispersed. (*To* MULLCANNY) Mother was th' oul' one who saved you from a sudden an' unprovided death. An' th' Blessed Image has come back again, all aglow in garments new. Listen !

[*A murmur of song has been heard while* AYAMONN *was speaking, and now* EEADA, DYMPNA, FINNOOLA, *and the* MEN *appear at the door — now wide open — half backing into the room singing part of a hymn softly, their pale faces still wearing the frozen look of resignation ; staring at the Image shining bright and gorgeous as* BRENNAN

75

*has made it for them, standing in a niche
in the wall, directly opposite the door.*
EEADA, DYMPNA, FINNOOLA, *and the* MEN
singing softly—

Oh ! Queen of Eblana's poor children,
Bear swiftly our woe away ;
An' give us a chance to live lightly
An hour of our life's dark day !
Lift up th' poor heads over bending,
An' light a lone star in th' sky,
To show thro' th' darkness, descending,
A cheerier way to die.

EEADA

(coming forward a little)

She came back to Her poor again, in raiment
rich. She came back ; of her own accord. She
came to abide with Her people.

DYMPNA

From her window, little Ursula looked, and saw
Her come ; in th' moonlight, along the street. She
came, stately. Blinded be the coloured light that
shone around about Her, the child fell back, in a
swoon she fell full on the floor beneath her.

1ST MAN

My eyes caught a glimpse of Her too, glidin'
back to where She came from. Regal an' proud
She was, an' wondrous, so that me eyes failed ;
me knees thrembled an' bent low, an' me heart
whispered a silent prayer to itself as th' vision

76

passed me by, an' I fancied I saw a smile on Her holy face.

EEADA

Many have lived to see a strange thing this favoured night, an' blessin' will flow from it to all tempered into a lively belief ; and maybe, too, to some who happen to be out of step with the many marchin' in the mode o' thruth. (*She comes a little closer to* MRS. BREYDON. *The others, backs turned towards the room, stand, most of them outside the door, a few just across the threshold, in a semicircle, heads bent as if praying, facing towards the Image.*) Th' hand of a black stranger it was who sent the stones flyin' through your windows ; but ere tomorrow's sun is seen, they will be back again as shelther from th' elements. A blessin' generous on yous all — (*pause*) — except th' evil thing that stands, all stiff-necked, underneath th' roof !

MULLCANNY
(mockingly)

Me !

SHEILA
(fiercely)

Ay, you, that shouldn't find a smile or an unclenched hand in a decent man's house !

MULLCANNY

I'll go ; there's too many here to deal with — I'll leave you with your miracle.

AYAMONN

You can stay if you wish, for whatever surety of

77

shelther's here, it's open to th' spirit seeking to add another colour to whatever thruth we know already. Thought that has run from a blow will find a roof under its courage here, an' a fire to sit by, as long as I live an' th' oul' rooms last!

SHEILA

(with quiet bitterness)

Well, shelter him, then, that by right should be lost in the night, a black night, an' bitterly lonely, without a dim ray from a half-hidden star to give him a far-away companionship; grey rain, in sodden showers, pouring over him; speary sleet slashing at his dead-cold face; numb limbs on him that must stir to keep alive, but can't move; with blanched fingers aching sorely from th' sting of a sharp wind; ay, an' a desolate rest under a thorny and dripping thicket of lean and twisted whins, too tired to thry to live longer against th' hate of the black wind and th' grey rain: Let him lie there, let him live there, forsaken, forgotten by all under a kindly roof and close to a cosy fire!

MULLCANNY

(with pretended alarm)

Good God, I'm done, now! I'm off before worse befall me. Good night, Ayamonn.

AYAMONN

Good night, my friend.   [MULCANNY *goes out*.

BRENNAN

We're keepin' decent people out of their beds — so long, all.

78

ROORY

I'll be with you some o' th' way, an' we can finish that argument we had. Good night all.

> [*He and* BRENNAN *go out together, closing the door after them.* SHEILA *stands where she was, sullen and silent.*

MRS. BREYDON

Shame on you, Sheila, for such a smoky flame to come from such a golden lamp ! (SHEILA *stays silent.*) Tired out I am, an' frightened be th' scene o' death I saw today. Dodge about how we may, we come to th' same end.

AYAMONN

(gently leading her towards the other room)
Go an' lie down, lady ; you're worn out. Time's a perjured jade, an' ever he moans a man must die. Who through every inch of life weaves a patthern of vigour an' elation can never taste death, but goes to sleep among th' stars, his withered arms outstretched to greet th' echo of his own shout. It will be for them left behind to sigh for an hour, an' then to sing their own odd songs, an' do their own odd dances, to give a lonely God a little company, till they, too, pass by on their bare way out. When a true man dies, he is buried in th' birth of a thousand worlds.

> [MRS. BREYDON *goes into the other room, and* AYAMONN *closes the door softly behind her. He comes back and stands pensive near the fire.*

79

AYAMONN
(*after a pause*)
Don't you think you should go too ?

SHEILA
(*a little brokenly*)
Let me have a few more words with you, Ayamonn,
before we hurry to our separation.

AYAMONN
(*quietly*)
There is nothing more to be said.

SHEILA
There's a lot to be said, but hasty time won't
stretch an hour a little out to let the words be
spoken.   Goodbye.

AYAMONN
(*without turning his head*)
Goodbye.
[SHEILA *is going slowly to the door when it
partly opens, and half the head of* EEADA
*peeps around it, amid an indistinct murmur
as of praying outside.*

EEADA
(*in half a whisper*)
Th' Protestan' Rector to see Mr. Breydon. (*The
half of her head disappears, but her voice is heard
saying a little more loudly*) This way, sir ; shure
you know th' way well, anyhow.
[*The door opening a little more, the* RECTOR

*comes in. He is a handsome man of forty.
His rather pale face wears a grave scholarly
look, but there is kindness in his grey eyes,
and humorous lines round his mouth,
though these are almost hidden by a short,
brown, pointed beard, here and there about
to turn grey. His black clothes are covered
by a warm black topcoat, the blackness
brightened a little by a vivid green scarf he
is wearing round his neck, the fringed ends
falling over his shoulders. He carries a
black, broad-brimmed, soft clerical hat and
a walking-stick in his left hand. He
hastens towards* AYAMONN, *smiling genially,
hand outstretched in greeting.*

RECTOR

My dear Ayamonn. (*They shake hands.*)

AYAMONN

(*indicating* SHEILA)

A friend of mine, sir—Sheila Moorneen. (*Moving
a chair.*) Sit down, sir.

[*The* RECTOR *bows to* SHEILA ; *she returns it
quietly, and the* RECTOR *sits down.*

RECTOR

I've hurried from home in a cab, Ayamonn, to
see you before the night was spent. (*His face
forming grave lines*) I've a message for you —
and a warning.

[*The door again is partly opened, and again
the half head of* EEADA *appears, mid the*

81

*murmurs outside, unheard the moment the
door closes.*

Two railwaymen to see you, Ayamonn; full
house tonight you're havin', eh?

[*The half head goes, the door opens wider,
and the two railwaymen come into the room.
They are dressed drably as the other men
are, but their peaked railway uniform caps
(which they keep on their heads) have vivid
scarlet bands around them. Their faces,
too, are like the others, and stonily stare in
front of them. They stand stock still when
they see the* RECTOR.

1ST RAILWAYMAN
(*after a pause*)

'Scuse us. Didn' know th' Protestan' Minister
was here. We'll wait outside till he goes,
Ayamonn.

AYAMONN

Th' Rector's a dear friend of mine, Bill; say
what you want, without fear — he's a friend.

1ST RAILWAYMAN
(*a little dubiously*)

Glad to hear it. You know th' sthrike starts
tomorrow?

AYAMONN

I know it now.

2ND RAILWAYMAN

Wouldn' give's th' extra shillin'. Offered us

82

thruppence instead — th' lowsers ! (*Hastily —
to* RECTOR) 'Scuse me, sir.

IST RAILWAYMAN
(*taking a document from his breast pocket*)
An' th' meetin's proclaimed.

RECTOR
(*to* AYAMONN)
That's part of what I came to tell you.

IST RAILWAYMAN
(*handing document to* AYAMONN)
They handed that to our Committee this evening,
a warrant of warning.

RECTOR
(*earnestly — to* AYAMONN)
I was advised to warn you, Ayamonn, that the
Authorities are prepared to use all the force they
have to prevent the meeting.

AYAMONN
Who advised you, sir — th' Inspector ?

RECTOR
My churchwarden, Ayamonn.   Come, even he
has good in him.

AYAMONN
I daresay he has, sir ; I've no grudge against him.

RECTOR
(*convinced*)
I know that, Ayamonn.

AYAMONN

(*indicating document — to* 1ST RAILWAYMAN)

What are th' Committee going to do with this?

1ST RAILWAYMAN

What would you do with it, Ayamonn?

AYAMONN

(*setting it alight at the fire and waiting till it
falls to ashes*)

That!

2ND RAILWAYMAN

(*gleefully*)

Exactly what we said you'd do!

SHEILA

(*haughtily*)

It's not what any sensible body would think he'd
do.

1ST RAILWAYMAN

(*ignoring her*)

Further still, Ayamonn, me son, we want you to
be one of the speakers on the platform at the
meeting.

SHEILA

(*bursting forward and confronting the railwaymen*)

He'll do nothing of the kind — hear me? Nothing
of the kind. Creepers, dead-faced desirers of a
life that can never enter into you, go! Cinder-
tongued moaners, who's to make any bones about
what you suffer, or how you die? Ayamonn's
his reading and his painting to do, and his mother

84

to mind, more than lipping your complaints in front of gun muzzles, ready to sing a short and sudden death-song !

1ST RAILWAYMAN
(a little awed)
To see Ayamonn we came, an' not you, Miss.

2ND RAILWAYMAN
(roughly)
Let th' man speak for himself.

AYAMONN
(catching SHEILA's arm and drawing her back)
It's my answer they're seeking. *(To railwaymen)*
Tell the Committee, Bill, I'll be there ; and that they honour me when they set me in front of my brothers. The Minstrel Show must be forgotten.

SHEILA
(vehemently — to the RECTOR)
You talk to him ; you're his friend. You can influence him. Get him to stay away, man !

RECTOR
It's right for me to warn you, Ayamonn, and you, men, that the Authorities are determined to prevent the meeting ; and that you run a grave risk in defying them.

2ND MAN
(growling)
We'll chance it.

85

SHEILA

(*to* RECTOR)

That's no good ; that's not enough — forbid him
to go.   Show him God's against it !

RECTOR

(*standing up*)

Who am I to say that God's against it ?   You
are too young by a thousand years to know the
mind of God.   If they be his brothers, he does
well among them.

SHEILA

(*wildly*)

I'll get his mother to bar his way.   She'll do more
than murmur grand excuses.

> [*She runs to the door of the other room, opens
> it, and goes in.   After a few moments, she
> comes out slowly, goes to the chair left idle
> by the* RECTOR, *sits down on it, leans her
> arms on the table, and lets her head rest on
> them.*

AYAMONN

Well ?

SHEILA

(*brokenly*)

She's stretched out, worn and wan, fast asleep,
and I hadn't the heart to awaken her.

RECTOR

(*holding out a hand to* AYAMONN)

Come to see me before you go, Ayamonn.   Be
sure, wherever you may be, whatever you may
do, a blessing deep from my breast is all around

86

you.   Goodbye.   (*To the railwaymen*) Goodbye,
my friends.

RAILWAYMEN

Goodbye, sir.

> [*The* RECTOR *glances at* SHEILA, *decides to say
> nothing, and goes towards the door ;*
> AYAMONN *opens it for him, and he goes out
> through the semicircle of men and women,
> still singing softly before the Statue of the
> Queen of Eblana's poor.* SHEILA's *quiet
> crying heard as a minor note through the
> singing.*

Oh, Queen of Eblana's poor children,
Bear swiftly our woe away,
An' give us a chance to live lightly,
An hour of our life's dark day !

CURTAIN

87

ACT III

Scene : *A part of Dublin City flowering into a street and a bridge across the river Liffey. The parapets are seen to the right and left so that the bridge fills most of the scene before the onlooker. The distant end of the bridge leads to a street flowing on to a point in the far distance ; and to the right and left of this street are tall gaunt houses, mottled with dubious activities, with crowds of all sorts of men and women burrowing in them in a pathetic search for a home. These houses stand along another street running parallel with the river. In the distance, where the street, leading from the bridge, ends in a point of space, to the right, soars the tapering silver spire of a church ; and to the left, Nelson's Pillar, a deep red, pierces the sky, with Nelson, a deep black, on its top, looking over everything that goes on around him. A gloomy grey sky is over all, so that the colours of the scene are made up of the dark houses, the brown parapets of the bridge, the grey sky, the silver spire, the red pillar, and Nelson's black figure.*

On one of the bridge parapets a number of the men seen in the previous scenes are gathered together, their expressionless faces hidden by being bent down towards their breasts. Some sit on the parapets, some lounge against the

88

gaunt houses at the corner of the street leading
from the bridge, and, in one corner, a man
stands wearily against the parapet, head bent,
an unlit pipe drooping from his mouth,
apparently forgotten. The sun shines on
pillar and church spire, but there is no sign
of sun where these people are.
On the pavement, opposite to where the men sit,
nearer to this end of the bridge, sit EEADA,
DYMPNA, *and* FINNOOLA, *dressed so in black*
that they appear to be enveloped in the black-
ness of a dark night. In front of EEADA *is a*
drab-coloured basket in which cakes and apples
are spending an idle and uneasy time. DYMPNA
has a shallower basket holding decadent
blossoms, and a drooping bunch of violets
hangs from a listless hand.

EEADA
(*drowsily*)

This spongy leaden sky's Dublin ; those tomby
houses is Dublin too — Dublin's scurvy body ;
an' we're Dublin's silver soul. (*She spits vigorously*
into the street.) An' that's what Eeada thinks of
th' city's soul an' body !

DYMPNA

You're more than right, Eeada, but I wouldn't
be too harsh. (*Calling out in a sing-song way*)
Violets, here, on'y tuppence a bunch ; tuppence a
bunch, th' fresh violets !

89

EEADA

(calling out in a sing-song voice)

Apples an' cakes, on'y tuppence a head here for
th' cakes ; ripe apples a penny apiece !

DYMPNA

Th' sun is always at a distance, an' th' chill grey
is always here.

FINNOOLA

Half-mournin' skies for ever over us, frownin'
out any chance of merriment that came staggerin'
to us for a little support.

EEADA

That's Dublin, Finnoola, an' th' sky over it.
Sorrow's a slush under our feet, up to our ankles,
an' th' deep drip of it constant overhead.

DYMPNA

A graveyard where th' dead are all above th'
ground.

EEADA

Without a blessed blink of rest to give them hope.
An' she cockin' herself up that she stands among
other cities as a queen o' counsel, laden with
knowledge, afire with th' song of great men,
enough to overawe all livin' beyond th' salty sea,
undher another sun be day, an' undher a different
moon be night.

[*They drowse, with heads bent lower.*

IST MAN

(leaning wearily against the parapet)

Golden Gander'll do it, if I'm e'er a thrue prophet.

(*Raising his voice a little*) He'll flash past th' winnin' post like an arra from th' bow, in the five hundhred guinea West's Awake Steeplechase Championship.

2ND MAN
(drowsily contradicting)

In me neck he will! He'd have a chance if it was a ramble. Copper Goose'll leave him standin', if I'm e'er a thrue prophet.

EEADA
(waking up slightly)

Prophets? Do me ears deceive me, or am I afther hearin' somebody say prophets?

DYMPNA

You heard a murmur of it, Eeada, an' it's a bad word to hear, remindin' us of our low estate at th' present juncture. Th' prophets we once had are well hidden behind God be now, an' no wondher, for we put small pass on them, an' God in His generous anger's showin' us what it is to be saddled with Johnnies-come-marchin'-home, all song an' shirt an' no surety.

FINNOOLA
(shaking her head sadly)

A gold-speckled candle, white as snow, was Dublin once; yellowish now, leanin' sideways, an' guttherin' down to a last shaky glimmer in th' wind o' life.

EEADA

Well, we've got Guinness's Brewery still, giv in

91

us a needy glimpse of a betther life an hour or so on a Saturday night, though I hold me hand at praisin' th' puttin' of Brian Boru's golden harp on every black porther bottle, destined to give outsiders a false impression of our pride in th' tendher an' dauntless memories of th' past. But it's meself should whisper little against th' bottles, havin' used them as cunnin' candlesticks, year in an' year out, since I lost meself in marriage ; an' a fine conthrast is a tall white candle, set firm in th' neck of a slender black bottle, givin' light to all in th' room, an' showin' up th' blessed St. Anthony himself, watchin' over us from a cosy corner in th' breast of the chimney.

> *The* RECTOR *and the* INSPECTOR *appear at the farther end of the bridge, and come over it towards where the men and women are. The* RECTOR *is dressed in immaculate black, wears a glossy tall hat, and carries a walking-stick. He has shed his topcoat, but wears his green scarf round his neck. The* INSPECTOR *is clad in a blue uniform, slashed with silver epaulettes on the shoulders, and silver braid on collar and cuffs. He wears a big blue helmet, back and front peaks silver-bordered, and from a long silver spike on the top flows a graceful plume of crimson hair. On the front is a great silver crown, throned on a circle of red velvet. A sword, in a silver scabbard, hangs by his side. He is wearing highly-polished top-boots. They both pause on the*

bridge, the RECTOR *looking pensively down over the parapet at the flowing river.*

INSPECTOR

It was a great wedding, sir. A beautiful bride and an elegant bridegroom ; a distinguished congregation, and the Primate in his fine sermon did justice to the grand occasion, sir. Fittingly ended, too, by the organ with *The Voice that Breathed o'er Eden.*

RECTOR
(apparently not very interested)

Oh yes, yes ; quite.

INSPECTOR

Historic disthrict, this, round here : headquarters of a Volunteer Corp in Grattan's time — not, of course, that I agree with Grattan. A great-great-grandfather of mine was one of the officers.

RECTOR

Oh yes ; was he ?

INSPECTOR

Yes. Strange uniform he wore : richly black, with sky-blue facings, a yellow breast-piece, ribbed with red braid, and, capping all, a huge silver helmet having a yellow plume soaring over it from the right-hand side.

RECTOR
(smiling)

Your own's not too bad, Mr. Churchwarden.

Smart ; but a bit too sombre, I think, sir.

EEADA

(*whining towards them*)

On'y a penny each, th' rosy apples, lovely for th'
chiselurs — Jasus ! what am I sayin' ? Lovely
for th' little masters an' little misthresses, stately,
in their chandeliered an' carpeted dwellin'-houses ;
or a cake — on'y tuppence a piece — daintily
spiced, an' tastin' splendid.

DYMPNA

(*whining towards them*)

Tuppence, here, th' bunch o' violets, fit for to go
with th' white an' spotless cashmere gown of our
radiant Lady o' Fair Dealin'.

EEADA

(*deprecatingly*)

What are you sayin', woman ? That's a Protestan'
ministher, indeed, gentleman, Dympna !

DYMPNA

Me mind slipped for a poor minute ; but it's pity
he'll have on us, an' regulate our lives with what'll
bring a sudden cup o' tea within fair reach of
our hands.

EEADA

Apples, here, penny each, rosy apples, picked
hardly an hour ago from a laden three ; cakes
tuppence on'y, baked over scented turf as th'

dawn stepped over th' blue-gowned backs o' th'
Dublin Mountains.

DYMPNA

Tuppence a bunch, th' violets, shy an' dhrunk
with th' dew o' th' mornin'; fain to lie in the
white bosom of a highborn lady, or fit into th'
lapel of a genuine gentleman's Sunday courtin'
coat.

    [*The* RECTOR *takes a few coins from his
    pocket and throws them to the women, who
    pick them up and sink into silence again.*

INSPECTOR

Swift, too, must have walked about here with the
thorny crown of madness pressing ever deeper
into his brain.

RECTOR

(*indicating the men and women*)

Who are these?

INSPECTOR

(*indifferent*)

Those? Oh, flotsam and jetsam. A few of them
dangerous at night, maybe; but harmless during
the day.

RECTOR

I've read that tens of thousands of such as those
followed Swift to the grave.

INSPECTOR

Indeed, sir? A queer man, the poor demented
Dean; a right queer man.

[*A sleepy lounger suddenly gives a cough, gives his throat a hawk, and sends a big spit on to one of the* INSPECTOR's *polished boots, then sinks back into sleep again.*

INSPECTOR
(*springing back with an angry exclamation*)
What th' hell are you after doing, you rotten lizard! Looka what you've done, you mangy rat!
[*He takes hold of the lounger and shakes him sharply.*

2ND MAN
(*sleepily resentful*)
Eh, there! Wha' th' hell?

INSPECTOR
(*furiously*)
You spat on my boots, you tousled toad — my boots, boots, boots!

2ND MAN
(*frightened and bewildered*)
Boots, sir? Is it me, sir? Not me, sir. Musta been someone else, sir.

INSPECTOR
(*shaking him furiously*)
You, you, you!

2ND MAN
Me, sir? Never spit in public in me life, sir. Makin' a mistake, sir. Musta been someone else.

RECTOR

Inspector Finglas! Remember you wear the King's uniform! Quiet, quiet, man!

INSPECTOR
(*subsiding*)

Pardon me. I lost my temper. I'm more used to a blow from a stone than a dirty spit on my boot.

RECTOR
(*shuddering a little*)

Let us go from here. Things here frighten me, for they seem to look with wonder on our ease and comfort.

INSPECTOR

Frighten you? Nonsense — and with me!

RECTOR

Things here are of a substance I dare not think about, much less see and handle. Here, I can hardly bear to look upon the same thing twice.

INSPECTOR

There you are, and as I've said so often, Breydon's but a neat slab of a similar slime.

RECTOR

You wrong yourself to say so: Ayamonn Breydon has within him the Kingdom of Heaven. (*He pauses.*) And so, indeed, may these sad things we turn away from.   [*They pass out.*

97

(thinking of the coins given)

Two tiny sixpences — fourpence a head. Oh, well, beggars can't be choosers. But isn't it a hard life to be grindin' our poor bums to powder, for ever squattin' on the heartless pavements of th' Dublin streets !

DYMPNA

Ah, what is it all to us but a deep-written testament o' gloom : grey sky over our heads, brown an' dusty streets undher our feet, with th' black an' bitther Liffey flowin' through it all.

EEADA

(mournfully)

We've dhrifted down to where there's nothin'. Younger I was when every quiet-clad evenin' carried a jaunty jewel in her bosom. Tormented with joy I was then as to whether I'd parade th' thronged sthreets on th' arm of a 16th Lancer, his black-breasted crimson coat a sight to see, an' a black plume droopin' from his haughty helmet ; or lay claim to a red-breasted Prince o' Wales's Own, th' red plume in his hat a flame over his head.

DYMPNA

It was a 15th King's Own Hussar for me, Eeada, with his rich blue coat an' its fairyland o' yellow braid, two yellow sthripes down his trousers, an' a red bag an' plume dancin' on his busby.

EEADA

Lancers for me, Dympna.

DYMPNA
Hussars for me, Eeada.

EEADA

An' what for you, Finnoola ?

FINNOOLA

What would a girl, born in a wild Cork valley,
among mountains, brought up to sing the songs
of her fathers, what would she choose but the
patched coat, shaky shoes, an' white hungry face
of th' Irish rebel ?   But their shabbiness was
threaded with th' colours from the garments of
Finn Mac Cool of th' golden hair, Goll Mac
Morna of th' big blows, Caoilte of th' flyin' feet,
an' Oscar of th' invincible spear.

EEADA

(*nudging* DYMPNA)

That was some time ago, if y'ask me.

> [BRENNAN *comes slowly over the bridge from
> the far side. His melodeon is hanging on
> his back. He looks around for a likely
> place to play. He leans against a parapet,
> some distance off, and unslings his melodeon
> from his back.*

EEADA

Here's that oul' miser creepin' after coppers,
an' some bank bulgin' with what he has in it
already.

2ND MAN

(waking suddenly, spitting out vigorously, and speaking venomously)

Rowlin' in th' coin o' th' realm — bastard ! (*He sinks into a coma again.*)

BRENNAN

(giving himself confidence)

Evenin', ladies an' gentlemen. Good thing to be alive when th' sun's kind. (*They take no heed of what he says.*)

[BRENNAN *sighs ; then plays a few preliminary notes on the melodeon to make sure it is in tune. He begins to sing in a voice that was once a mellow baritone, but now is a little husky with age, now and again quavering a little on the higher notes in the song.*

BRENNAN

(singing)

I stroll'd with a fine maid far out in th'
   counthry,
Th' blossoms around us all cryin' for dew ;
On a violet-clad bench, sure, I sat down beside
   her,
An' tuck'd up my sleeves for to tie up her shoe.
An' what's that to anyone whether or no,
If I came to th' fore when she gave me th'
   cue ?
She clos'd her eyes tight as she murmur'd
   full low,
Be good enough, dear, for to tie up my shoe.

EEADA
(*with muttered indignation*)
Isn't that outrageous, now ; on a day like this, too, an' in a sober mood !

DYMPNA
In front o' decent women as well !

IST MAN
(*waking up suddenly*)
Disturbin' me dhreams of Golden Gandher gallopin' home to win in a canther !

BRENNAN
(*singing*)
Th' hawthorn shook all her rich perfume upon
us,
Red poppies saluted, wherever they grew,
Th' joyous exertion that flaunted before me,
When I tuck'd up my sleeves for to fasten her
shoe.
An' what's it to anyone, whether or no ?
I learn'd in that moment far more than I knew,
As she lifted her petticoat, shyly an' slow,
An' I tuck'd up my sleeves for to fasten her
shoe.

The heathery hills were all dancin' around us,
False things in th' world turn'd out to be
thrue,
When she put her arms round me, an' kiss'd
me an' murmur'd,
You've neatly an' tenderly tied up my shoe.

What's that to anyone whether or no ?
I ventur'd quite gamely to see th' thing
   through,
When she lifted her petticoat, silent an' slow,
An' I tuck'd up my sleeves for to tie up her
   shoe.

[*Some pennies have been thrown from the
windows of the houses.* BRENNAN *picks
them up and, taking off a shabby, wide-
brimmed hat, bestows a sweeping bow on
the houses. During the singing of the last
verse of the song,* AYAMONN *and* ROORY *have
strolled in, and have listened to the old man
singing while they leant against the balus-
trade of the bridge. The scene has grown
darker as the old man is singing his song,
for the sun is setting.*

2ND MAN
(*waking up suddenly*)

Off with you, old man, thinkin' to turn our
thoughts aside from th' way we are, an' th' worn-
out hope in front of us.

1ST MAN
(*waking up — wrathfully*)

Get to hell outa that, with your sootherin' songs
o' gaudy idleness !

EEADA

Makin' his soul, at his age, he ought to be,
instead o' chantin' ditties th' way you'd fear what

would come upon you in th' darkness o' th' night,
an' ne'er a sword be your side either.

Away with you an' your heathen songs to parts
renowned for ignorance an' shame !

FINNOOLA
Away to where light women are plenty, an' free
to open purple purses to throw you glitterin'
coins !
[BRENNAN *slings his melodeon on to his back,
puts his hat back on his head, and wends
his way across the bridge.*

ROORY
(*as he passes*)
Isn't it a wondher, now, you wouldn't sing an
Irish song, free o' blemish, instead o' one thickly
speckled with th' lure of foreign enthertainment ?
[BRENNAN *heeds him not, but crosses the bridge
and goes out. The men and women begin
to sink into drowsiness again.*

AYAMONN
Let him be, man ; he sang a merry song well,
and should have got a fairer greeting.

ROORY
(*taking no notice of* AYAMONN's *remark — to
the men and women*)
Why didn't yous stop him before he began ?
Pearl of th' White Breasts, now, or *Battle Song*

103

o' Munster that would pour into yous Conn's battle-fire of th' hundhred fights. Watchman o' Tara he was, his arm reachin' over deep rivers an' high hills, to dhrag out a host o' sthrong enemies shiverin' in shelthers. Leadher of Magh Femon's Host he was, Guardian of Moinmoy, an' Vetheran of our river Liffey, flowin' through a city whose dhrinkin' goblets once were made of gold, e'er wise men carried it with frankincense an' myrrh to star-lit Bethlehem.

EEADA

(*full of sleep — murmuring low*)

Away you, too, with your spangled memories of battle-mad warriors buried too deep for words to find them. Penny, here, each, th' ripe apples.

DYMPNA

(*sleepily — in a low murmur*)

Away, an' leave us to saunter in sleep, an' crave out a crust in the grey kingdom of quietness. Tuppence a bunch the fresh violets.

FINNOOLA

(*sleepily*)

Run away, son, to where bright eyes can see no fear, an' white hands, idle, are willin' to buckle a sword on a young man's thigh.

IST MAN

(*with a sleepy growl*)

Get to hell where gay life has room to move, an' hours to waste, an' white praise is sung to coloured shadows. Time is precious here.

2ND AND 3RD MEN
(together — murmuringly)
Time is precious here.

AYAMONN
Rouse yourselves ; we hold a city in our hands !

EEADA
(in a very low, but bitter voice)
It's a bitther city.

DYMPNA
(murmuring the same way)
It's a black an' bitther city.

FINNOOLA
(speaking the same way)
It's a bleak, black, an' bitther city.

1ST MAN
Like a batthered, tatthered whore, bullied by too long a life.

2ND MAN
An' her three gates are castles of poverty, penance, an' pain.

AYAMONN
She's what our hands have made her. We pray too much and work too little. Meanness, spite, and common pattherns are woven thick through all her glory ; but her glory's there for open eyes to see.

EEADA
(bitterly — in a low voice)
Take your fill of her glory, then ; for it won't

last long with your headin' against them who hold the kingdom an' who wield th' power.

DYMPNA
(*reprovingly*)
He means well, Eeada, an' he knows things hid from us; an' we know his poor oul' mother's poor feet has worn out a pathway to most of our tumbling doorways, seekin' out ways o' comfort for us she sadly needs herself.

EEADA
(*in a slightly livelier manner*)
Don't I know that well! A shabby sisther of ceaseless help she is, blind to herself for seein' so far into th' needs of others. May th' Lord be restless when He loses sight of her!

FINNOOLA
For all her tired look an' wrinkled face, a pure white candle she is, blessed this minute by St. Colmkille of th' gentle manner, or be Aidan, steeped in th' lore o' Heaven, or be Lausereena of th' silver voice an' snowy vestments — th' blue cloak o' Brigid be a banner over her head for ever!

THE OTHER TWO WOMEN
(*together*)
Amen.

ROORY
(*impatiently*)
We waste our time here — come on!

106

AYAMONN

Be still, man ; it was dark when th' spirit of God first moved on th' face of th' waters.

ROORY

There's nothin' movin' here but misery. Gun peal an' slogan cry are th' only things to startle them. We're useless here. I'm off, if you're not.

AYAMONN

Wait a moment, Roory. No-one knows what a word may bring forth. Th' leaves an' blossoms have fallen, but th' three isn't dead.

ROORY
(*hotly*)

An' d'ye think talkin' to these tatthered second-hand ghosts'll bring back Heaven's grace an' Heaven's beauty to Kaithleen ni Houlihan ?

AYAMONN

Roory, Roory, your Kaithleen ni Houlihan has th' bent back of an oul' woman as well as th' walk of a queen. We love th' ideal Kaithleen ni Houlihan, not because she is false, but because she is beautiful ; we hate th' real Kaithleen ni Houlihan, not because she is true, but because she is ugly.

ROORY
(*disgusted*)

Aw, for God's sake, man !

[*He hurries off angrily.*

EEADA
(*calling scornfully after him*)
God speed you, scut !

AYAMONN
(*placing a hand softly on* EEADA's *head*)
Forget him, an' remember ourselves, and think
of what we can do to pull down th' banner from
dusty bygones, an' fix it up in th' needs an'
desires of today.

> [*The scene has now become so dark that things
> are but dimly seen, save the silver spire and
> the crimson pillar in the distance ; and
> AYAMONN's head set in a streak of sunlight,
> looking like the severed head of Dunn-Bo
> speaking out of the darkness.*

FINNOOLA
Songs of Osheen and Sword of Oscar could do
nothing to tire this city of its shame.

AYAMONN
Friend, we would that you should live a greater
life ; we will that all of us shall live a greater
life. Our sthrike is yours. A step ahead for us
today ; another one for you tomorrow. We who
have known, and know, the emptiness of life
shall know its fullness. All men and women
quick with life are fain to venture forward.
(*To* EEADA) The apple grows for you to eat. (*To*
DYMPNA) The violet grows for you to wear. (*To*
FINNOOLA) Young maiden, another world is in
your womb.

108

EEADA

(*still a little gloomily*)

Th' soldiers will be chasin' us with gunfire ; th' polis hoppin' batons off our heads ; our sons an' husbands hurried off to prison, to sigh away th' time in gloomier places than those they live in now.

AYAMONN

Don't flinch in th' first flare of a fight. (*He looks away from them and gazes meditatively down the river.*) Take heart of grace from your city's hidden splendour. (*He points with an outstretched hand.*) Oh, look ! Look there ! Th' sky has thrown a gleaming green mantle over her bare shoulders, bordhered with crimson, an' with a hood of gentle magenta over her handsome head — look !

> [*The scene has brightened, and bright and lovely colours are being brought to them by the caress of the setting sun. The houses on the far side of the river now bow to the visible world, decked in mauve and burnished bronze ; and the men that have been lounging against them now stand stalwart, looking like fine bronze statues, slashed with scarlet.*

AYAMONN

Look ! Th' vans an' lorries rattling down th' quays, turned to bronze an' purple by th' sun, look like chariots forging forward to th' battle-front.

[EEADA, *rising into the light, now shows a fresh
   and virile face, and she is garbed in a dark-
   green robe, with a silvery mantle over her
   shoulders.*

EEADA
(*gazing intently before her*)
Shy an' lovely, as well as battle-minded !
[DYMPNA *rises now to look where* AYAMONN *is
   pointing. She is dressed like* EEADA, *and
   her face is aglow. The men have slid from
   the parapets of the bridge, turning, too, to
   look where* AYAMONN *is pointing. Their
   faces are aglow, like the women's, and they
   look like bronze statues, slashed with a
   vivid green.* FINNOOLA *rises, last, and
   stands a little behind the others, to look at
   the city showing her melody of colours.*
   FINNOOLA *is dressed in a skirt of a brighter
   green than the other two women, a white
   bodice slashed with black, and a flowing
   silvery scarf is round her waist.*

FINNOOLA
She's glowin' like a song sung be Osheen himself,
with th' golden melody of his own harp helpin' !

IST MAN
(*puzzled*)
Something funny musta happened, for, 'clare to
God, I never noticed her shinin' that way before.

2ND MAN
Looka the loungers opposite have changed to

sturdy men of bronze, and th' houses themselves
are gay in purple an' silver !

Our tired heads have always haunted far too low
a level.

AYAMONN
There's th' great dome o' th' Four Courts lookin'
like a golden rose in a great bronze bowl ! An'
th' river flowin' below it, a purple flood, marbled
with ripples o' scarlet ; watch th' seagulls glidin'
over it — like restless white pearls astir on a royal
breast. Our city's in th' grip o' God !

1ST MAN
(*emotionally*)
Oh, hell, it's grand !

EEADA
Blessed be our city for ever an' ever.

AYAMONN
(*lifting his right hand high*)
Home of th' Ostmen, of th' Norman, an' th' Gael,
we greet you ! Greet you as you catch a passing
hour of loveliness, an' hold it tightly to your
panting breast ! (*He sings.*)
    Fair city, we tell thee our souls shall not
        slumber
    Within th' warm folds of ambition or gain ;
    Our hands shall stretch out to th' fullness of
        labour,
    Till wondher an' beauty within thee shall
        reign.

111

(singing together)

We vow to release thee from anger an' envy,
To dhrive th' fierce wolf an' sly fox from thy
  gate,
Till wise men an' matrons an' virgins shall
  murmur
O city of splendour, right fair is thy fate !

AYAMONN
(singing)

Fair city, I tell thee that children's white
  laughter,
An' all th' red joy of grave youth goin' gay,
Shall make of thy streets a wild harp ever
  sounding,
Touch'd by th' swift fingers of young ones at
  play !

THE REST
(singing)

We swear to release thee from hunger an'
  hardship,
From things that are ugly an' common an'
  mean ;
Thy people together shall build a brave city,
Th' fairest an' finest that ever was seen !

[FINNOOLA *has been swaying her body to the
  rhythm of the song, and now, just as the
  last part is ending, she swings out on to
  the centre of the bridge in a dance. The
  tune, played on a flute by someone, some·*

*where, is that of a Gavotte, or an air of some
dignified and joyous dance, and, for a while,
it is played in fairly slow time. After some
time it gets quicker, and* AYAMONN *dances out
to meet her. They dance opposite each other,
the people around clapping their hands to
the tap of the dancers' feet. The two move
around in this spontaneous dance, she in a
golden pool of light, he in a violet-coloured
shadow, now and again changing their
movements so that she is in the violet-
coloured shadow, and he in the golden pool.*

EEADA
(*loudly*)

The finest colours God has to give are all around
us now.

FINNOOLA
(*as she dances*)

The Sword of Light is shining !

1ST MAN
(*exultantly*)

Sons an' daughters of princes are we all, an' one
with th' race of Melesius !

[*The dance comes to an end with* AYAMONN
and FINNOOLA *having their arms round
each other.*

EEADA

Praise God for th' urge of jubilation in th' heart
of th' young.

113

An' for th' swiftness of leg an' foot in th' heart of a dance.

2ND MAN

An' for th' dhream that God's right hand still holds all things firmly.

> [*The scene darkens slightly.* AYAMONN *loosens his hold on* FINNOOLA *and raises his head to listen to something. In the distance can be heard the sound of many feet marching in unison.*

FINNOOLA
(a little anxiously)

What is it you're listenin' to?

AYAMONN

I must go; goodbye, fair maid, goodbye.

FINNOOLA

Is it goin' to go you are, away from the fine things shinin' around us? Amn't I good enough for you?

AYAMONN
(earnestly)

You're lovely stayin' still, an' brimmin' over with a wilder beauty when you're dancin'; but I must go. May you marry well, an' rear up children fair as Emer was, an' fine as Oscar's son; an' may they be young when Spanish ale foams high on every hand, an' wine from th' royal Pope's a common dhrink! Goodbye.

> [*He kisses her, and goes across the bridge,*

*passing out of sight on the farther bank of
the river. The figures left behind have
shrunk a little ; the colours have faded a
good deal, and all look a little puzzled and
bewildered. The loungers have fallen back
to the walls of the houses, and, though they
do not lie against them, they stand close to
them, as if seeking their shelter. There is
a fairly long pause before anyone speaks.
They stand apart, as if shy of each other's
company.*

EEADA
(murmuringly)

Penny each, th' ripe apples. Who was that spoke
that time ? Jasus ! I musta been dhreamin'.

DYMPNA
(in a bewildered voice)

So must I, th' way I thought I was lost in a
storm of joy, an' many colours, with gay clothes
adornin' me.

FINNOOLA
(puzzled and dreamy)

Dhreamin' I musta been when I heard strange
words in a city nearly smothered be stars, with
God guidin' us along th' banks of a purple river,
all of us clad in fresh garments, fit to make Osheen
mad to sing a song of the revelry dancin' in an' out
of God's own vision.

EEADA
(murmuringly, but a little peevishly)

Fot God's sake give over dwellin' on oul' songs

115

sung be Osheen, th' way you'd be kindlin' a fire o' glory round some poor bog-warbler chantin' hoarse ditties in a shelthered corner of a windy street. (*Very sleepily*) Th' dewy violets, here, on'y tuppence a bunch.

[*Now the tramp-tramp of marching men is heard more plainly.*

DYMPNA
(*a little more awake*)
What can that be, now ?

1ST MAN
(*gloomily, but with a note of defiance in his voice*)
Th' thramp of marchin' soldiers out to prevent our meetin' an' to stop our sthrike.

2ND MAN
(*in a burst of resolution*)
We'll have both, in spite of them !

[*The scene darkens deeply now. In the pause following the 2ND MAN's remark, nothing is heard but the sound of the tramping feet ; then through this threatening sound comes the sound of voices singing quietly, voices that may be of those on and around the bridge, or of those singing some little distance away.*

VOICES
(*singing quietly*)
We swear to release thee from hunger and
    hardship,

From things that are ugly and common and
 mean ;
The people together shall build a great city,
The finest and fairest that ever was seen.

CURTAIN

ACT IV

Scene : *Part of the grounds surrounding the Protestant church of St. Burnupus. The grounds aren't very beautiful, for they are in the midst of a poor and smoky district; but they are trim, and, considering the surroundings, they make a fair show. An iron railing running along the back is almost hidden by a green and golden hedge, except where, towards the centre, a fairly wide wooden gate gives admittance to the grounds. Beyond this gateway, on the pathway outside, is a street lamp. Shrubs grow here and there, and in the left corner, close to the hedge, are lilac and laburnum trees in bloom. To the right is the porch of the church, and part of the south wall, holding a long, rather narrow window, showing, in coloured glass, the figures of SS. Peter and Paul. Some distance away from the porch is a rowan tree, also in blossom, its white flowers contrasting richly with the gay yellow of the laburnum and the royal purple of the lilac. The rest of the grounds are laid out in grass, except for the path leading from the gateway to the entrance of the church. It is a warm, sunny evening, the Vigil of Easter, and the* RECTOR *is sitting on a deck-chair, before a table, on which are some books and papers. He is evidently con-*

118

*sidering the services that are to be held in the
church on the following day.*

The RECTOR *is wearing a thick black cassock
lined with red cloth, and at the moment is
humming a verse of a hymn softly to himself,
as he marks down notes on a slip of paper
before him. A square black skull-cap covers
his head.*

RECTOR
(*singing to himself, softly*)

As Thou didst rise from Thy grim grave,
So may we rise and stand to brave
Th' power bestow'd on fool or knave ;
We beseech Thee !

[*The verger comes out from the porch and walks
towards the* RECTOR. *He is bald as an egg,
and his yellowish face is parched and
woebegone-looking. He is a man of sixty,
and shows it. His ordinary clothes are
covered with a long black mantle of thin
stuff, with a small cape-like addition or
insertion of crimson velvet on the shoulders.*

RECTOR
(*noticing the verger beside him*)

Hymn 625 : we must have that as our opening
hymn, Samuel.

SAMUEL
It's got to go in, sir.

RECTOR
As you say — it's got to go in. Did you want to
speak to me, Samuel ?

SAMUEL

Excuse me, sir, for what I'm agoin' to say.

RECTOR

(*encouragingly*)

Yes, yes, Samuel, go on.

SAMUEL

(*mysteriously*)

Somethin's afther happenin', sir, that I don't like.

RECTOR

(*turning a little in his chair*)

Oh ! What's that, Sam ?

SAMUEL

Mr. Fosther was here this mornin' runnin' a hand through th' daffodils sent for Easther, an' found somethin' he didn't like

RECTOR

Yes ?

SAMUEL

It's not for me to remark on anything that manœuvres out in front o' me, or to slip in a sly word on things done, said, or thought on, be th' pastors, masthers, or higher individuals of th' congregation ; but, sometimes, sir, there comes a time when a true man should, must speak out.

RECTOR

(*with a sigh*)

And the time has come to say something now — what is it, Sam ?

SAMUEL

(in a part whisper)

This mornin', sir, and th' dear spring sun shinin' through th' yellow robes of Pether an' th' purple robes o' Paul, an' me arrangin' th' books in th' pews, who comes stealin' in, but lo and behold you, Fosther an' Dowzard to have a squint round. Seein' they're Select Vesthrymen, I couldn't ask them why they were nosin' about in th' silence of th' church on an ordinary week-day mornin'.

RECTOR

(patiently)

Yes ; but a long time ago, you said something about daffodils.

SAMUEL

I'm comin' at a gallop to them, sir.

RECTOR

Good ; well, let's hear about the daffodils.

SAMUEL

Aha, says I, when I seen th' two prowlers with their heads close together, whisperin', aha, says I, there's somethin' on th' carpet.

RECTOR

Is what you have to tell me something to do with Dowzard and Foster, or the daffodils ?

SAMUEL

Wait till you hear ; sometimes Fosther an' Dowzard'll be to th' fore, an' sometimes th' daffodils. What can these two oul' codgers be up to, says I, sidlin' up to where they were, hummin' a hymn.

RECTOR

Humming a hymn ? I'm glad to hear it ; for I'd be surprised to hear either of them humming a hymn.

SAMUEL

Me it was, sir, who was hummin' th' hymn ; for in a church, I like me thoughts to go with th' work I'm doin', if you know what I mean.

RECTOR
(*impatiently*)

It'll be nightfall before you get to the daffodils, man.

SAMUEL

Wait till you hear, sir. There I was gettin' close to them be degrees, when, all of a sudden, didn't Fosther turn on me, shoutin' " Are you goin' to be a party to th' plastherin' of Popish emblems over a Protestan' church ? "

RECTOR

Popish emblems ?

SAMUEL

Th' daffodils, sir.

RECTOR

The daffodils ? But they simply signify the new life that Spring gives ; and we connect them in a symbolic way, quite innocently, with our Blessed Lord's Rising. And a beautiful symbol they are : daffodils that come before the swallow dares, and take the winds of March with beauty. Shake-speare, Sam.

SAMUEL

(*lifting his eyes skywards and pointing upwards*)
Altogether too high up for poor me, sir. (*He
bends down close to the* RECTOR's *ear*.) When he
seen the cross o' daffodils made be Breydon, he
near went daft. (*A pause, as if* SAMUEL *expected
the* RECTOR *to speak, but he stays silent*.) God
knows what'll be th' upshot if it's fixed to the
Communion Table, sir. (*Another slight pause*.)
Is it really to go there, sir ? Wouldn't it look a
little more innocent on th' pulpit, sir ?

RECTOR
(*in a final voice*)
I will place it myself in front of the Communion
Table, and, if Mr. Foster or Mr. Dowzard ask
anything more about it, say that it has been
placed there by me. And, remember, when you
say Mr. Foster and Mr. Dowzard, it's to be Mr.
Breydon too. (*He hands some leaflets to* SAMUEL.)
Distribute these through the pews, Sam, please.
The arranging of the flowers is finished, is it ?

SAMUEL
Yessir ; all but the cross.

RECTOR
I will see to that myself. Thanks, Sam.
   [SAMUEL *goes off into the church, and the*
      RECTOR, *leaning back in his chair with a
      book in his hand, chants softly.*

123

RECTOR

(*chanting*)

May wonders cease when we grow tame,
Or worship greatness in a name ;
May love for man be all our fame,
We beseech Thee !

> [*As he pauses to meditate for a moment,* MRS.
> BREYDON *is seen coming along, outside the
> hedge.   She enters by the gate, and comes
> over to the* RECTOR.   SHEILA *has come with
> her, but lags a little behind when they enter
> the grounds.   The* RECTOR *rises quickly
> from his chair to greet* MRS. BREYDON.

RECTOR

(*warmly*)

My dear Mrs. Breydon !   Hasn't it been a lovely
day ?   The weather promises well for Easter.

MRS. BREYDON

It would be good if other things promised as well
as the weather, sir.

RECTOR

We must be patient, and more hopeful, my friend.
From the clash of life new life is born.

MRS. BREYDON

An' often new life dies in th' clash too.   Ah,
when he comes, sir, speak th' word that will keep
my boy safe at home, or here.

RECTOR

(*laying a gentle hand on her arm*)

I wish I could, dear friend ;   I wish I could.

His mind, like his poor father's, hates what he sees as a sham ; an' shams are powerful things, mustherin' at their broad backs guns that shoot, big jails that hide their foes, and high gallows to choke th' young cryin' out against them when th' stones are silent.

RECTOR

Let those safely sheltered under the lawn of the bishop, the miniver of the noble, the scarlet and ermine of the judge, say unto him, this thing you must not do ; I won't, for sometimes out of the mouths of even babes and sucklings cometh wisdom.

SHEILA

If what's against him be so powerful, he is help-less ; so let this power go on its way of darkened grandeur, and let Ayamonn sit safe by his own fireside.

[*To the left, on the path outside the hedge, the* INSPECTOR, *in full uniform, appears, evidently coming to see the* RECTOR *; on the right, followed by the men and women of the previous scenes, appears* AYAMONN. *He and the* INSPECTOR *meet at the gate. The* INSPECTOR *and he halt. The* INSPECTOR *indicates he will wait for* AYAMONN *to pass, and* AYAMONN *comes into the grounds towards the* RECTOR. *The* INSPECTOR *follows, but, in the grounds, stands a little apart, nearer the hedge. The men and women spread along the path outside, and*

*stay still watching those in the grounds
from over the hedge. They hold themselves
erect, now ; their faces are still pale, but
are set with seams of resolution. Each is
wearing in the bosom a golden-rayed sun.*
BRENNAN *comes in and, crossing the grass,
sidles over to sit down on the step of the
porch.*

RECTOR
(*shaking* AYAMONN'*s hand*)
Ah, I'm so glad you've come ; I hope you'll stay.

AYAMONN
(*hastily*)
I come but to go.   You got the cross of daffodils ?

RECTOR
Your mother brought it to us ; it will hang in
front of our church's greatest promise.   Come and
place it there with your own loyal hands,
Ayamonn.

INSPECTOR
Loyal hands engaged in rough rending of the
law and the rumpling-up of decency and order ;
and all for what ?   For what would but buy
blacking for a pair of boots, or a sheet of glass to
mend a broken window !

BRENNAN
(*from his seat on the porch's step*)
He's right, Ayamonn, me son, he's right :
money's the root of all evil.

AYAMONN
(*to the* INSPECTOR)
A shilling's little to you, and less to many ; to us
it is our Shechinah, showing us God's light is near;
showing us the way in which our feet must go ;
a sun-ray on our face ; the first step taken in the
march of a thousand miles.

INSPECTOR
(*threateningly*)
I register a lonely warning here that the people
of power today will teach a lesson many will
remember for ever ; though some fools may not
live long enough to learn it.

MRS. BREYDON
Stay here, my son, where safety is a green tree
with a kindly growth.

MEN AND WOMEN
(*in chorus — above*)
He comes with us !

SHEILA
Stay here where time goes by in sandals soft,
where days fall gently as petals from a flower,
where dark hair, growing grey, is never noticed.

MEN AND WOMEN
(*above*)
He comes with us !

AYAMONN
(*turning towards them*)
I go with you !

INSPECTOR

(*vehemently*)

Before you go to carry out all your heated mind is set to do, I warn you for the last time that today swift horses will be galloping, and swords will be out of their scabbards !

RECTOR

(*reprovingly — to* INSPECTOR)

I hope you, at least, will find no reason to set your horses moving.

INSPECTOR

(*stiffly*)

I'll do my duty, sir ; and it would be a good thing if someone we all know did his in that state of life unto which it has pleased God to call him.

RECTOR

(*losing his temper*)

Oh, damn it, man, when you repeat the Church's counsel, repeat it right ! Not *unto which it has pleased God to call him*, but *unto which it shall please God to call him*.

INSPECTOR

(*losing his temper too*)

Damn it, man, do you believe that what the fellow's doing now is the state of life unto which it has pleased God to call him ?

RECTOR

(*hotly*)

I have neither the authority nor the knowledge

128

to deny it, though I have more of both than you, sir !

[*The* INSPECTOR *is about to answer angrily, but* SHEILA *catches his arm.*

SHEILA

Oh, cancel from your mind the harder things you want to say, an' do your best to save us from another sorrow !

INSPECTOR

(*shaking off* SHEILA'*s hand roughly, and going to the gateway, where he turns to speak again*)
Remember, all ! When swords are drawn and horses charge, the kindly Law, so fat with hesitation, swoons away, and sees not, hears not, cares not what may happen.

MRS. BREYDON
(*angrily — up to the* INSPECTOR)
Look at th' round world, man, an' all its wondhers, God made, flaming in it, an' what are you among them, standing here, or on a charging horse, but just a braided an' a tasselled dot !
[*The* INSPECTOR *hurries off, to pause, and stands outside the hedge, to the right, the men and women shrinking back a little in awe to give him a passage.*

MRS. BREYDON
(*to* AYAMONN)
Go on your way, my son, an' win. We'll welcome another inch of the world's welfare.

RECTOR

(*shaking his hand*)

Go, and may the Lord direct you ! (*He smiles.*)
The Inspector's bark is louder than his bite is
deep.

AYAMONN

For the present — goodbye !

[AYAMONN *hurries away through the gate,
pausing, outside the hedge to the left,
turning to give a last look at the* INSPECTOR.

INSPECTOR

Bear back, my boy, when you see the horsemen
charging !

[*He goes out by the right, and* AYAMONN *goes
out left, followed by the men and the women.
There is a slight pause.*

RECTOR

(*briskly — to banish a gloomy feeling*)

Now, Mrs. Breydon, you run along to the vestry,
and make us a good cup of tea — I'm dying for
one. (*To* SHEILA) You'll join us, Miss Moorneen,
won't you ?

SHEILA

(*immediately anxious*)

Oh no, thanks. I . . . I shouldn't even be here.
I'm a Catholic, you know.

RECTOR

I know, and I'd be the last to ask you do anything you shouldn't ; but rest assured there's no
canonical law against taking tea made by a

Protestant. Off you go, and help Mrs. Breydon.
I'll join you in a moment.

> [SHEILA *and* MRS. BREYDON *go off by the south
> wall of the church.*

BRENNAN
(*as the* RECTOR *is gathering his books and papers
from the table*)
Hey, sir ; hey there, sir : It won't shatther th'
community at large this disturbance, will it, eh ?

RECTOR
I hope not.

BRENNAN
(*with a forced laugh*)
No, no, of course not. Bank of Ireland'll still
stand, eh ? Ay. Ravenous to break in, some of
them are, eh ? Ay, ay. Iron doors, iron doors
are hard to open, eh ?

RECTOR
(*going off to get his tea*)
I suppose so.

BRENNAN
Ay, are they. He supposes so ; only supposes —
there's a responsible man for you !

> [*The verger comes into the porch and bends
> over* BRENNAN.

SAMUEL
(*in a hoarse whisper*)
Come in an' have a decko at our grand cross.

Cross ?   What cross ?

SAMUEL

One o' daffodils ; for Easther ; to be put in front
o' th' Communion Table.

BRENNAN

(*climbing as quick as he can from the porch step*)
Popery, be God ! We'll put a spoke in that wheel.
Lemme in to see.

    [*He goes into the church with the verger, who
      closes the door. After a pause, the sound of
      running feet is heard at a distance, and some
      stones hop off the path outside the hedge. In
      a few moments* DOWZARD *and* FOSTER *come
      running along, hurry through the gateway
      and pause, breathless, beside the porch.* DOW-
      ZARD *is a big, beefy, red-faced man, rolls of
      flesh pouring out over the collar of his coat.
      His head is massive and bald, with jet-
      black tufts behind his ear, and a tiny fringe
      of it combed across high over his forehead.
      *FOSTER *is small and scraggy, with aggres-
      sion for ever lurking in his cranky face,
      ready to leap into full view at the slightest
      opportunity. His cheeks and lips are
      shaven, but spikes of yellowish whiskers
      point defiantly out from under his chin.
      His voice is squeaky and, when it is
      strengthened in anger, it rises into a thin
      piping scream. Both are dressed in the*

*uniforms of railway foremen, blue cloth,
with silver buttons, and silver braid on*
DOWZARD's *peaked hat and coat-sleeves, and
gold braid on those of* FOSTER. *Both have
their coats tightly buttoned up on them.
They take off their peaked caps and wipe
sweat from their foreheads.* DOWZARD
pushes the door.

DOWZARD
(*panting*)

Door shut, blast it! We're safe here, though, in
th' grounds; Church grounds sacred. Unguarded,
verminous villains — Papists, th' lot o' them!

FOSTER
(*venomously*)

On' one o' their leaders a Select Vestryman. On'
thot domned Rector stondin' by him. Steeped in
Popery: sign o' th' cross; turnin' eastward
sayin' th' Creed; sung Communion — be Gud,
it's a public scondal!

DOWZARD

Some o' them stones scorched me ear passin' by.
We shouldn't have worn our uniforms. Gave us
away. I knew we were in for it when they called
us scabs.

FOSTER
(*going over and sitting down by the table*)

Scobs themselves! Smoky, vonomous bastards!
Sut down, mon, on' calm yourself. I tull you I'd

133

wear me uniform in th' Vutican. (*He unbuttons his coat and shows that he is wearing a vivid orange sash, bordered with blue.*) Thor's me sash for all tae see. You should ha' stud with me, mon ; stud like th' heroes o' Dully's Brae !

[*The men and women run in, crouchingly, from right and left. They make the movement of throwing stones at the two men, who are hit on the head, and fall over the table as if they had been stunned, while the men and women raise their voices in a song, led by the* IST MAN, *all standing behind the hedge.*

IST MAN
(*singing*)
If we can't fire a gun, we can fire a hard stone,
Till th' life of th' scab shrivels into a moan.

REST
(*in chorus*)
Let it sink in what I say,
Let me say it again—
Though th' Lord God made an odd scab, sure,
He also made men !

IST MAN
(*singing*)
There's room in this big world for Gentile an' Jew,
For th' Bashibazouk, but there's no room for you ;

REST
(*in chorus*)

Let it sink in what I say,
Let it sink in what I tell—
You'll be lucky to find a spare place down in
hell !

1ST MAN
(*singing*)

Th' one honour you'll get is a dusty black
plume
On th' head of th' nag taking you to th' tomb.

REST
(*in chorus*)

Let it sink in what I say,
Let it sink in what I tell—
Th' scab's curs'd be th' workers, book, candle,
an' bell !

[*As they sing the last part of the last verse,
they move away, those on the right, to the
left ; and those on the left, to the right.
After a short pause,* DOWZARD, *holding a
hand to his head, staggers over to the church
door and kicks violently at it.*

DOWZARD
(*shouting*)

Ey, there, in there, come out, open th' blasted
door an' help a half-dead man !

[*The church door is opened, and the* RECTOR,
followed by the verger and BRENNAN, *comes
out into the grounds.*

RECTOR

What's wrong ; what has happened ?

DOWZARD

Th' Pope's bullies with hard stones have smitten us sore. Honest men, virtuous an' upright, loyal to th' law an' constitution, have this day been smitten sore with Popish stones — oh, me poor head !

FOSTER

St. Bartholomew's Day's dawnin' again, I'm tullin' yous, an' dismumbered Protestants'll lie on all th' sthreets !

RECTOR
(*to the verger*)

Run in and fetch a basin of water, and tear a few strips from the old surplice hanging in the press. (*The verger goes back to the church, and the* RECTOR *turns to the two men.*) You can't be badly hurt when you complain so grandly.

FOSTER
(*indignantly*)

Thot's right — pooh-pooh away a loyal Protestant skull all but shotthered to buts be a Popish stone !

RECTOR

Let me see the damage done. (*He examines the wound.*) Ah, a slight contusion. You won't die a martyr yet. (*The verger returns with basin of water and strips of linen, and the* RECTOR *bathes and bandages* FOSTER's *head.*) There, you'll do nicely. (*To* DOWZARD) Now for yours. (*He*

136

examines the wound.) Not even as bad as Mr. Foster's. (*He bathes and bandages* DOWZARD'S *wound.*) Your caps saved you both from worse injuries.

FOSTER

Stand up for th' ruffians be makin' luttle of our hurts, so do, ay, do. (*Noticing* BRENNAN *who has edged towards the gate and is about to go away.*) Eh, you, aren't you goin' to stay an' put tustimony to the fullness ó' th' Protestan' feth?

BRENNAN
(*with slight mockery*)

Ay, I would, an' welcome, if I hodn't to go, forbye, at this hour of on uvery day, I mak' ut a rule tae be sturdy in th' readin' of a chapther o' God's word so's I won't hold on tae wordly things too strongly.   [*He goes out.*

FOSTER
(*fiercely*)

A jully-fush Protestant! (*To the* RECTOR) Look see, I tull you th' fires o' Smithfield 'ull be blazin' round Protestant bodies again, an' coloured lights 'ull be shown in th' Vatican windows soon!

DOWZARD

An' we'll be th' first to go up in th' flames.

RECTOR
(*laughing contemptuously*)

Nonsense, oh, nonsense.

137

FOSTER

(*almost screaming*)

It's not nonsense, mon ! Every sable-robed
Jesuit's goin' about chucklin', his honds twitchin'
to pounce out on men like me here, an' Eddie
Dowzard there, tae manacle us, head, hond, and
fut, for th' wheel, th' thumbscrew, an' th' rack,
an' then finish us up at th' stake in a hoppy
Romish auto-dey-fey ! The Loyola boyos are out
to fight another buttle with th' men o' King Bully!

RECTOR

(*amused*)

Well, let the Loyola boyos and King Bully fight
it out between them. I'm too busy to join either
side. Goodbye.

FOSTER

(*catching his arm as he is going — viciously*)

You're no' goin' tae be lut slide off like thot, now,
with your guilty conscience, mon. There's things
to be done, and things tae be ondone in yon
church, there ; ay, ay.

RECTOR

(*quietly*)

Indeed ?

FOSTER

(*angrily — to* DOWZARD)

Uh, speak, speak a word, mon, on' don't leave
ut all tae me.

DOWZARD

First, sir, we want you to get rid o' Breydon from
the Vesthry an' from th' church.

RECTOR

Oh, indeed ?

FOSTER

(*almost screaming*)

It's no' oh, indeed ; answer th' question — plain
yes or no !

RECTOR

(*coldly*)

Gentlemen, Mr. Breydon stays in the Vestry till
the parishioners elect someone else ; as for the
church, God has seen fit to make him a member
of Christ, and it is not for me, or even for you,
gentlemen, to say that God did wrong.

DOWZARD

(*sneeringly*)

An' when did that wondherful thing hoppen ?

RECTOR

At his baptism, as you yourself should know.

FOSTER

(*with an agonised squeal*)

Popery, popery, nothin' but popery ! Th' whole
place's infusted with it !

[*The verger appears at the porch door with
the cross of daffodils in his hand. It has a
Keltic shape, the shafts made of the flowers,
and the circle of vivid green moss. The
verger shows it to* DOWZARD, *behind the*
RECTOR's *back, and* DOWZARD *sidling over,
takes it from him, the verger returning into
the church again.*

139

And now be good enough, Mr. Foster, to let go my arm.

FOSTER

(*still gripping the* RECTOR's *arm, and now thrusting his distorted face closer to the* RECTOR's)

You're thryin' to make a Mass-house of God's tumple ; you'd like to do a donce with th' whore o' Babylon, if we'd lot yeh, th' whore in purple an' scorlet, an' dhrunk with th' blood o' th' saints, if we lot yeh !

DOWZARD

(*dancing out in front of them holding out the (cross — with exultant anger*)

There y'are, see ? Caught in the very act — red-handed — a popish symbol flourished in th' faces of Protestant people ! (*With a shout*) Ichabod, Ichabod !

FOSTER

(*dancing about as if he were a dancing dervish*)

Things done behind our bocks are done in front of our faces ! Oh, th' sly, sleek, sacerdutal, jesuitical worshippers of a wafer god ! I'll no' stick it, no ; I'll no' stick it. Looksee, the rage godly, kindling Luther, kindles me ! Down with them thot inflame th' hearts o' th' congregation with th' sight o' Romish images ! Here, go gimme a holt o' thot. (*He snatches the cross of flowers from* DOWZARD, *flings it on the ground, and dances wildly on it.*) Th' Bible on' th' Crown ; th' twa on a half ; th' orange on' blue ; on' th'

Dagon o' Popery ondher our feet ! Protestonts,
Protestonts, up on' be doin' !

DOWZARD
(*wildly shouting*)
Th' dhrum, th' dhrum, th' Protestant dhrum !
[*While* FOSTER *and* DOWZARD *have been
dancing about and shouting their last few
words, the men and women have run
frightened along the path, behind the hedge.
Those running from the right, turn, and
run back to the left ; those running from
the left, turn, and run back to the left again,
passing each other as they run.*

FOSTER
(*frantically*)
We'll die, give up th' ghost, suffer onything tae
save ceevil on' reeligious liberty ! (*He suddenly
sees the men and women running about behind the
hedge, and at once plunges into the porch, almost
knocking the* RECTOR *down, and is followed, just
as swiftly, by* DOWZARD. *As he flies — to the*
RECTOR) Out uh th' way, mon, out uh th' way !
[EEADA *comes running through the gate, into
the garden, over to the* RECTOR.

EEADA
(*beseechingly*)
Oh, sir, please let me into the church, till all th'
sthrife is over — no place's safe with the soldiers
firin' an' th' police runnin' mad in a flourish o'
batons !

141

RECTOR

(*reassuringly*)

Be calm, be quiet, they won't touch a woman. They remain men, however furious they may be for the moment.

EEADA

Ara, God help your innocence ! You should ha' seen them sthrikin' at men, women, an' childher. An' me own friend, Dympna, in hospital gettin' her face laced with stitches, th' way you'd lace a shoe ! An' all along of followin' that mad fool, Breydon !

RECTOR

Go in, then. (*To the verger, who has come to the entrance*) See her safe.

> [EEADA *and the verger go into the church. A man, led by the* 1ST MAN, *whose face is full of fright and strain, comes through the gate into the grounds. The man has a huge brass tuba hammered down over his head, and, now and again, a faint moan is heard coming from beneath it.*

1ST MAN

(*irritably — to man whose head is covered by the tuba*)

Oh, for God's sake lift your feet an' look where you're goin'. Show your paces, or we'll both be ornaments for the morgue ! (*Dragging him into the ground*s.) Here, in here, till th' danger's past.

(*exultantly, coming out of porch with* DOWZARD)
Aha, you're no' firin' stones, now, at decent
Christian people !

DOWZARD
(*standing pompously in their path*)
Off with you somewhere else, you Papish ruffians !
Away with you from where men honour love,
peace, ordher, an' a Christian life.

RECTOR
(*coming forward and quietly setting* DOWZARD *aside*)
I'd better take control here ; these ignorant
people would never understand the purity of your
Christian affection. (*Firmly*) They will find
shelter here, till the law regains its temper. (*To*
IST MAN — *indicating tuba*) Who did this to that
poor man ?

IST MAN
(*trying to repress amusement*)
Horse police, sir : chargin' th' band, one o' them
stooped over, whipped th' big bugle out of his
hand, brought it down with a wallop over his
head, an' dhrove it home with his baton ; an' th'
rest, in passin', each had a skelp to fix it tighter.
(*Bending over to whisper in the* RECTOR'*s ear, he
explodes into a laugh.*) 'Clare to God, it'll take a
charge o' dynamite to get it off comfortable !

RECTOR
(*severely*)
It's nothing to joke about, my man. Are we to
make merry over another man's misery ?

143

(*apologetically*)

Oh, no; no, no. Sure, he can't hear me, sir.
A man makin' a joke of it deserves hangin'.
(*Breaking out again*) Doesn't he look, for all th'
world, like an oulden knight in golden armour
goin' out to conquer haythen kingdoms!

RECTOR
(*trying to move the tuba, and failing*)
I don't know what to do.

> [*The man with the tuba sinks down on the
> grass and lies there. Along the path, out-
> side the hedge, another frightened man
> comes running, and when he enters the
> gateway it is seen that the shell of a drum
> is fixed round his body. From his shoulders
> to his waist, his arms wedged within the
> shell as if in a vice, a green flag, with a
> golden harp on it, is laced to the drum's
> rim, so that it forms a kind of a short
> skimpy skirt down to the man's knees. He
> runs as quick as he can across the grounds,
> bumping against* FOSTER *as he passes, into
> the porch, and he can be heard kicking at
> the inner door ; then he comes to the outer
> door, to stand there and glare at all who are
> looking at him.*

MAN
(*with drum round him*)
Eh, there, will yous get this other door opened,
if yous don't want to see a man murdhered. Quit

your starin', will yous ?   Oh, isn't there one decent, honest, dear Christian left livin' to set me free from this helplessness before any oncomin' emergency !

IST MAN
(*choking with suppressed enjoyment*)
He's like th' Lady of th' Lake on th' banks of Loch Lomond — oh, th' polis's doin' mighty things to-day for the glory o' God an' th' honour of Ireland !

[*As the* 2ND MAN *leans helplessly against the side of the porch,* FINNOOLA *comes slowly along the path outside the hedge, holding on to the railings as she moves, step by step. When she comes to the gateway, she sinks down to the ground and turns a white and distorted face towards those in the grounds.*

FINNOOLA
(*painfully*)
For th' love o' God, one of you tell me if th' Reverend something Clinton's here, or have I to crawl a long way further ?

RECTOR
(*hurrying over to her*)
He's here ; I'm he, my good woman.   What is it you want of me ?

FINNOOLA
I've a message for you from Ayamonn Breydon.

RECTOR
(*eagerly*)
Yes, yes ; where is he ?

145

He's gone.

RECTOR

Gone ? Gone where ?

FINNOOLA

Gone to God, I hope. (*A rather long pause.*)

RECTOR
(*in a low voice*)
May he rest in peace !   And the message ?

FINNOOLA

Yes.   He whispered it in me ear as his life fled through a bullet-hole in his chest — th' soldiers, th' soldiers.   He said this day's but a day's work done, an' it'll be begun again tomorrow.   You're to keep an eye on th' oul' woman.   He wants to lie in th' church tonight, sir.   Me hip's hurt ; th' fut of a plungin' horse caught me, an' I flat on th' ground.   He sent a quick an' a long farewell to you.   Oh, for Christ's sake get's a dhrink o' wather !   (*The verger runs for a drink.*)   We stood our groun' well, though.   (*The verger comes back with the water, and she drinks.*)   Now I can have a thrickle of rest at last.   (*She stretches herself out on the ground.*)

RECTOR

Where did you leave him ?   Where is he lying now ?

[*She lies there, and makes no answer.   He picks up the broken cross of flowers and is silent for a few moments.*

146

RECTOR

(with head bent low — sorrowfully)

Oh, Ayamonn, Ayamonn, my dear, dear friend.
Oh, Lord, open Thou mine eyes that I may see
Thee, even as in a glass, darkly, in all this mis-
chief and all this woe !

[*The curtain comes down to indicate the
passing of some hours. When it rises again,
it is evening. The lamp over the porch door
is lighted, and so is the church, the light
shining through the yellow robe of St.
Peter and the purple robe of St. Paul from
the window in the church's wall. The
church organ is playing, very softly, a
dead march. The lamp on the path, outside
the hedge, isn't yet lighted. The dark
figures of men and women can be faintly
seen lining themselves along the hedge.*
MRS. BREYDON *is standing in the grounds,
near to the gateway.* FOSTER *and* DOWZARD
*stand on the steps of the porch. A little in
front, with his back turned towards them,
stands the* RECTOR, *now with white surplice
over his cassock, his stole around his neck,
and the crimson-lined hood of a Doctor of
Divinity on his shoulders.* SHEILA, *holding
a bunch of crimson roses in her hand, stands
under the rowan tree. Partly behind the
tree, the* INSPECTOR *is standing alone.
A* LAMPLIGHTER *comes along the path,
carrying his pole with the little flower of
light in the brass top. He lights the lamp*

on the path, then comes over to peer across the hedge.

LAMPLIGHTER

What's up ? What's on ? What's happenin'
here ? What'r they all doin' now?

IST MAN

Bringin' th' body o' Breydon to th' church.

LAMPLIGHTER

Aw, is that it ? Guessed somethin' was goin' on.

IST MAN

He died for us.

LAMPLIGHTER

Looka that, now ! An' they're all accouthered in
their best to welcome him home, wha' ? Aw, well,
th' world's got to keep movin', so I must be off;
so long ! [*He goes.*

DOWZARD

(*speaking to the* RECTOR's *back*)

For th' last time, sir, I tell you half of the Vestry's
against him comin' here ; they don't want our
church mixed up with this venomous disturbance.

RECTOR

(*without moving, and keeping his eyes looking
towards the gateway*)

All things in life, the evil and the good, the
orderly and disorderly, are mixed with the life of
the Church Militant here on earth. We honour
our brother, not for what may have been an error

148

in him, but for the truth for ever before his face. We dare not grudge him God's forgiveness and rest eternal because he held no banner above a man-made custom.

FOSTER

(*savagely*)

Aw, looksee, I'm no' a mon to sut down on' listen to a tumblin' blether o' words — wull ye, or wull ye not, give intil us ?

[*In the distance a bagpipe is heard playing* Flowers of the Forest. MRS. BREYDON's *body stiffens, and* SHEILA's *head bends lower on her breast.*

RECTOR

It is a small thing that you weary me, but you weary my God also. Stand aside, and go your way of smoky ignorance, leaving me to welcome him whose turbulence has sunken into a deep sleep, and who cometh now as the waters of Shiloah that go softly, and sing sadly of peace.

[*As he is speaking, the lament ceases, and a moment after, a stretcher bier, bearing the covered-up body of* AYAMONN, *appears at the gateway. It is carried down towards the church, and the* RECTOR *goes to meet it.*

RECTOR

(*intoning*)

Lord, Thou hast been our refuge from one generation to another. For a thousand years in Thy sight are but as yesterday. (*He chants.*)

149

All our brother's mordant strife,
Fought for more abundant life ;
For this, and more — oh, hold him dear.
Jesu, Son of Mary, hear !

Gather to Thy loving breast
Ev'ry laughing thoughtful jest,
Gemm'd with many a thoughtful tear.
Jesu, Son of Mary, hear !

When Charon rows him nigh to shore,
To see a land, ne'er seen before,
Him to rest eternal steer.
Jesu, Son of Mary, hear !

[*The bier is carried into the church, and, as
it passes,* SHEILA *lays the bunch of crimson
roses on the body's breast.*

SHEILA

Ayamonn, Ayamonn, my own poor Ayamonn !

[*The* RECTOR *precedes the bier, and* MRS.
BREYDON *walks beside it, into the church,
the rest staying where they are. There is a
slight pause.*

DOWZARD

We'd betther be goin . Th' man's a malignant
Romaniser. Keep your eye on th' rabble goin'
out.

FOSTER
(*contemptuously*)

There's little fight left in thom, th' now. I'll no'
forgive thot Inspector fur refusin' to back our
demond.

[*They swagger out through the gateway and
disappear along the path outside the hedge,
as those who carried the bier come out of
the church.*

2ND MAN

That's the last, th' very last of him — a core o'
darkness stretched out in a dim church.

3RD MAN

It was a noble an' a mighty death.

INSPECTOR

(*from where he is near the tree*)
It wasn't a very noble thing to die for a single
shilling.

SHEILA

Maybe he saw the shilling in th' shape of a new
world.

[*The* 2ND AND 3RD MEN *go out by the gateway
and mingle with the rest gathered there.
The* INSPECTOR *comes closer to* SHEILA.

INSPECTOR

Oughtn't you to go from this gloom, Sheila?
Believe me, I did my best. I thought the charge
would send them flying, but they wouldn't budge;
wouldn't budge, till the soldiers fired, and he was
hit. Believe me, I did my best. I tried to force
my horse between them and him.

SHEILA

(*calmly*)
I believe you, Inspector Finglas.

INSPECTOR

(*gently catching her by the arm*)

Tom to you, dear. Come, Sheila, come, and let
us put these things away from us as we saunter
slowly home.

SHEILA

(*with a quiver in her voice*)

Oh, not now ; oh, not tonight ! Go your own
way, and let me go mine, alone tonight.

INSPECTOR

(*taking her hand in his*)

Sheila, Sheila, be sparing in your thought for
death, and let life smile before you. Be sparing
in thought of death on one who spent his life too
rashly and lost it all too soon. Ill-gotten wealth
of life, ill-gone for ever !

SHEILA

(*withdrawing her hand from his gently*)

Oh, Tom, I hope you're right ; you are right,
you must be right.

> [*They have walked to the gateway, and now
> stand there together, the men and women
> along the hedge eyeing them, though pre-
> tending to take no notice.*

INSPECTOR

You'll see it clearer, dear, when busy Time in
space has set another scene of summer's glory,
and new-born spring's loud voice of hope hushes
to silence th' intolerant dead.

SHEILA
(*musingly*)

He said that roses red were never meant for me;
before I left him last, that's what he said. Dear
loneliness tonight must help me think it out, for
that's just what he said. (*Suddenly — with
violence*) Oh, you dusky-minded killer of more
worthy men!

[*She runs violently away from him, and goes
out, leaving him with the men and women,
who stand idly by as if noticing nothing.*

INSPECTOR
(*after a pause*)

What are ye doing here? Get home! Home
with you, you lean rats, to your holes and haunts!
D'ye think th' like o' you alone are decked with
th' dark honour of trouble? (*Men and women
scatter, slowly and sullenly, till only* BRENNAN,
*with his melodeon on his back, is left, leaning by
the gate. To* BRENNAN) Heard what I said?
Are you deaf, or what?

BRENNAN
(*calmly*)

I'm a Protestant, an' a worshipper in this church.

INSPECTOR

One of the elect! So was Breydon. Well, keep
clear of unruly crowds — my men don't wait to
ask the way you worship when they raise their
arms to strike.

[He goes slowly away down the path. A few moments pass, then the RECTOR *and* MRS. BREYDON *come out of the church. He arranges a shawl round her shoulders.*

RECTOR

There ; that's better ! My wife insists you stay the night with us, so there's no getting out of it.

MRS. BREYDON

She's kind. (*She pauses to look at the rowan tree.*) There's th' three he loved, bare, or dhrenched with blossom. Like himself, for fine things grew thick in his nature ; an' lather come the berries, th' red berries, like the blood that flowed today out of his white body. (*Suddenly — turning to face the church.*) Is it puttin' out th' lights he is ?

RECTOR

Yes, before he goes home for the night.

MRS. BREYDON

Isn't it a sad thing for him to be lyin' lonesome in th' cheerless darkness of th' livelong night !

RECTOR

(*going to the porch and calling out*)

Sam, leave the lights on tonight.

[The church, which had dimmed, lights up again.

RECTOR

He's not so lonesome as you think, dear friend,

but alive and laughing in the midst of God's gay
welcome. Come.

> [*They slowly go through the gate and pass
> out. The verger comes from the church
> and swings the outer door to, to lock up
> for the night.* BRENNAN *comes down into
> the grounds.*

SAMUEL

(*grumbling*)

Light on all night — more of his Romanisin'
manœuvres.

BRENNAN

Eh, eh, there ; houl' on a second !

SAMUEL

What th' hell do you want ?

BRENNAN

Just to sing a little song he liked as a sign of
respect an' affection ; an' as a finisher-off to a
last farewell.

SAMUEL

(*locking the door*)

An what d'ye take me for ? You an' your song
an' your last farewell !

BRENNAN

(*giving him a coin*)

For a bare few minutes, an' leave th' door open so's
th' sound'll have a fair chance to go in to him.
(*The verger opens the door.*) That's it. You're a
kind man, really.

> [BRENNAN *stands facing into the porch, the*

155

verger leaning against the side of it.
BRENNAN *unslings his melodeon, plays a few preliminary notes on it, and then sings softly.*

A sober, black shawl hides her body entirely,
Touch'd be th' sun an' th' salt spray of th'
  sea ;
But deep in th' darkness a slim hand, so
  lovely,
Carries a rich bunch of red roses for me !
  [*The rest of the song is cut off by the ending of the play.*

CURTAIN

RED ROSES FOR ME

A so-ber black shawl hides her bod-y en-ti-re-ly Touch'd by the
sun and th' salt spray of th' sea; But down in th' dark-ness a
slim hand so love-ly, Car-ries a rich bunch of red ro-ses for me.—

TH' BOULD FENIAN MEN

Our cour-age so ma-ny have thought to be ag-in', Now
flames like a bril-liant new star in the sky; An' Dan-ger is proud to be
call'd a new bro-ther, Since Freedom has buckled her sword on her thigh. Then
out to th' place where the bat-tle is brav-est, Where th'
noblest an' meanest fight fierce in th' fray, Re-pub-lic-an ban-ners shall
mock at th' foe-men, An' Fen-ians shall turn a dark night in-to day!

OH, QUEEN OF EBLANA'S POOR CHILDREN

Oh, Queen of Eb - la-na's poor child - ren, Bear swift - ly our woe a -

way; An' give us a chance to live light - ly An hour of our life's dark

day; Lift up th' poor heads ev - er bend - ing, An' light a lone star in th'

sky, To show thro' th' dark-ness, de-scend - ing, A cheer-i-er way to die.

I TUCK'D UP MY SLEEVES

I stroll'd with a fine maid far out in th' coun-try, Th'

blos - soms a - round us all cry - in' for dew;— On a

dai-sy deckt bench, sure, I sat down be-side her And tuck'd up my sleeves for to

tie up her shoe; An' what's that to a - ny one wheth-er or no, If I

came to th' fore when she gave me th' cue? She clos'd her eyes tight as she

mur-mured full low, Be good e-nough, dear, for to tie up my shoe.

158

FAIR CITY

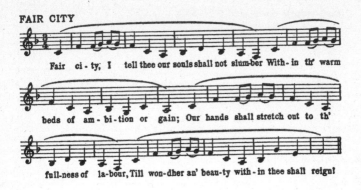

Fair ci - ty, I tell thee our souls shall not slum-ber With- in th' warm beds of am - bi - tion or gain; Our hands shall stretch out to th' full-ness of la-bour, Till won-dher an' beau-ty with - in thee shall reign!

WE BESEECH THEE

As Thou didst rise from Thy— grim grave, So may we rise to stand and brave Th' pow'r be - stow'd on fool — or knave.— We be - seech Thee!

THE SCAB

If we can't fire a gun, we can fire a hard stone, Till th' life of th' scab shriv-els in-to a moan. Let it sink in what I say, Let me say it a - gain— Tho' th' Lord God made an odd scab He al - so made men!

BROTHERS

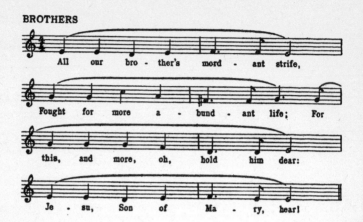

All our bro - ther's mord - ant strife,

Fought for more a - bund - ant life; For

this, and more, oh, hold him dear:

Je - su, Son of Ma - ry, hear!